BLUE & WHITE *at home*

BLUE & WHITE *at home*

INSPIRING SCHEMES FOR VINTAGE, COASTAL & COUNTRY INTERIORS

HENRIETTA HEALD

RYLAND PETERS & SMALL
LONDON • NEW YORK

Senior designer Megan Smith
Senior commissioning editor
  Annabel Morgan
Editor Sophie Devlin
Picture research Jess Walton
Head of production Patricia Harrington
Creative director Leslie Harrington

Published in 2022 by
Ryland Peters & Small
20–21 Jockey's Fields
London WC1R 4BW
and
341 E 116th Street
New York, NY 10029

www.rylandpeters.com

Text, design and photographs
© Ryland Peters & Small 2022

10 9 8 7 6 5 4 3 2 1

ISBN 978-1-78879-441-1

A CIP record for this book is available
from the British Library.

Library of Congress CIP data has been
applied for.

Printed and bound in China

CONTENTS

Introduction   6

VINTAGE   12

A New Take on Studio Blues   16
Vintage Fabrics   22
Peace at the Water's Edge   26
Delft Tiles   34
Glassware   36
Feast for the Eyes   38
Bathrooms   46
French Style in California   50
Enamelware   56
Lighting   58
Breton Inspirations   60
Furniture Blues   68

COASTAL   70

Fisherman's Cottage   74
Outdoor Living   80
Natural Serenity   84
Bedrooms   92
History Recaptured   96
Pattern   104
White Space Opening Up to the Sea   108
Display & Collections   114
Rescued From Extinction   118
Walls & Ceilings   124
Flooring   128

RUSTIC   130

Farmhouse Simplicity   134
Pigments & Dyes   142
A Dream of Old England   146
Kitchens & Dining   152
Danish Summer Cottage   156
Ceramics   162
A Fresh Look at Country Style   166
Garden Retreats   172
Calm After the Storm   176
Decorating with Flowers   184

Resources   186
Picture credits   188
Index   190
Acknowledgments   192

Introduction

Before starting to write this book, I had a good look around the interior of my north London home – and saw it with fresh eyes. It was amazing to discover how much blue there was. I realized that, quite unconsciously, I had become what one of the owners interviewed here describes as 'a blue-and-white addict'. And great fun it is too! This is not only an interior-design phenomenon. My car is blue, many of my clothes include elements of blue, even my yoga equipment is blue. I know that I'm not alone in this pleasant affliction. In surveys of the most popular colours, blue almost always comes out on top.

Having lived for years with subdued dusky pinks and sage greens – perfectly traditional in an early-19th-century terraced/row house – I decided to splash out and paint my entrance hallway bright aquamarine from floor to ceiling, while keeping the ceiling and skirting boards/baseboards white. Now, as you come through the front door, it's like diving underwater in a swimming pool, and new visitors to the house always comment on it.

The aquamarine theme is taken up in the dining room, where cabinet doors and shelves are painted the same colour. I have been even more adventurous there by choosing cobalt blue – which I like to call Matisse blue – for the walls above dado/chair-rail height. Below, the walls were kept white because of the concern that a room painted entirely cobalt would have been just too intense.

Elsewhere in the house, there are blue chevron-patterned rugs, blue floral and striped fabrics and plenty of sky-blue woodwork/trim. But my pride and joy is the diverse collection of blue-and-white plates, bowls, jugs/pitchers and other

ceramic objects amassed during my travels in various European countries. Some of these are used for practical purposes; others are hung on walls or displayed on shelves.

As vividly illustrated by the houses featured in this book – Vintage, Coastal and Rustic – the decorative opportunities offered by combining blue and white are virtually endless. And it is a practice that has been popular since ancient times. The colour pairing has been seen in, for example, wall and ceiling mosaics excavated at Pompeii, southern Italy, dating from the first century AD, and in other sites around the Mediterranean, whose inhabitants were doubtless inspired by the cerulean skies and azure seas of their native lands. Meanwhile, the earliest scientifically proven use of indigo as a dye for fabrics was 6,000 years ago in Peru.

In addition to showcasing a spectacular array of homes where decorative blues and whites predominate, from California to Spain to South Africa, *Blue & White At Home* includes special features on everything from vintage fabrics, ceramics and furniture to bedrooms, bathrooms, kitchens and outdoor living.

Henrietta Heald

Vintage

An ancient English farmhouse, a prairie home in northern California
and a traditional Breton mansion on a rocky bluff... these very different
properties are linked by two common themes: interiors that celebrate
the timeless combination of blue and white, and owners with a love
of all things vintage. The stories of five historical homes are told here
alongside special features on bathrooms, vintage fabrics and furniture,
Delft tiles, glassware, enamelware and more.

A NEW TAKE ON STUDIO BLUES

London-based antiques dealer Katharine Pole, a specialist in French textiles from the 18th to the mid 20th century, has a passion for all things indigo – ranging from printed and woven cloths to Provençal quilts, toiles, chintzes and indiennes. Her many imaginative recycling ventures include using old deadstock denim from a jeans factory to cover a sofa and an armchair.

Katharine is also drawn to rustic linens and fabrics that have had a former utilitarian purpose. 'As well as chateau curtains and silk bedcovers,' she says, 'I am happy buying the everyday linens and hemp that were used, for example, to collect olives or to add a layer between a straw-filled mattress and a sheet.'

A decade ago, Katharine and her husband moved into a Victorian terraced house in north-west London with the aim of combining a home with a studio/showroom. The previous owners had been a family of builders, who ended up doing the restoration work. They put in a new kitchen and two bathrooms, and removed all the existing flooring to reveal old wooden boards. 'We had seen many badly renovated period houses,' says Katharine, 'so it was very exciting to find somewhere that, despite the laminated floors in

TALKING POINT
Occupying pride of place in the showroom is an 18th-century four-poster piled high with quilts and cushions/pillows (*left & opposite*) – often the biggest talking point when clients visit. The awning and hangings are of a linen-and-silk fabric striped in red and beige, with double scallops edged in pale yellow silk. An old filing chest stands by the bed (*above*).

Combining a home with a studio can result in a lot of overflow into hallways and other rooms, but in spite of the challenges, Katharine loves her work environment. In the characterful showroom, fabric-covered boxes in faded hues (*left*) are stacked beside books, many devoted to the history of fashion and art. Blue is the unifying theme throughout the house, in both furnishing fabrics and garments on display, dominated by the French *biaude* clothing that was once rustic workwear (*opposite*). The sofa and antique chair in the living room (*below*) have been reupholstered in 1970s denim, with bold red stripes of a 19th-century woollen fabric added for greater impact.

the kitchen and some bedrooms, had plenty about it that was untouched and *dans son jus*, to use an expression favoured by French antiques dealers.' Fitted bedroom cabinets made way for wardrobes/armoires and chests of drawers/dressers.

The couple decided to retain as much as possible of the original character of the place: 'We loved the stair banisters as they had always been, with layers of paint and a slightly scuffed look.' In the upstairs room now used as a studio and display space, the former occupants had stripped one side wall of its old floral wallpaper to reveal the terracotta-hued plaster beneath. This was kept, and the back wall was given the same treatment, leaving either side of the fireplace wallpapered, creating a sympathetic backdrop for showcasing textiles, many of them patched and frayed.

Katharine's quilts are notable for their gently repetitive palette, with indigo, off-white and dusky pink as recurring themes. Her love of indigo dates from childhood, when she and her family lived in northern Nigeria, and she has

vivid memories of the Tuareg guards of their living compound wearing magnificent indigo turbans as they sat around drinking mint tea. Now she collects and sells French *biaude* clothing – traditional linen smocks worn by peasants and farm workers as they went about their business. Originally darkest blue, these garments have faded to attractive lighter shades after many years of wear and laundering.

While the upstairs showroom is rich in layers of colour and texture, the downstairs rooms have an air of calm. White walls and natural floorboards set off a few special items of furniture, many given an unexpected twist. In the living room, indigo contrasts beautifully with other colours and the soft whites of a 19th-century sofa upholstered in hemp. Dark sofa and chair covers made from recycled denim are teamed with antique French and Swedish blue-and-white-striped cushions/pillows to achieve a lightening effect.

FRENCH INFLUENCES
Vintage textiles, mostly sourced from France, are stacked up on an old patisserie stand (*top left*) or given a new lease of life as cushion/pillow covers (*above*). The indigo-dyed parasols (*top right*) were once used by French shepherds to protect them from the sun. Drawers of a former filing chest made from a denim-blue canvas material are now used to store scraps of fabric (*opposite*). The hatbox and bonnet, both in a washed-out blue, date from the early 19th century, and the same shades are picked out in the portrait and dried flowers.

Vintage Fabrics

Textiles that feel most at home in a vintage setting are those with a story of their own to tell. These range from antique fabrics that embody the irregularities and subtleties of age to modern reproductions of, for example, old French toiles and Asian ikats.

Even scraps of old materials or offcuts from larger pieces can have a powerful impact when repurposed as cushion/pillow covers, throws or table runners. Artfully chosen textiles – whether in the form of curtains, blinds/shades or accessories, or used on chairs, sofas or beds – can lift every other element in a room.

Silks, tapestries and damasks have been used as furnishing fabrics since ancient times, as have indigo dyes, the earliest known example of which was discovered in 6,000-year-old cotton textiles from Peru.

Damask silks were favoured as wall coverings in the 18th century, and papers printed with damask designs are still used to adorn walls, but such expensive items are generally seen in only the grandest homes. Much more widespread now in furnishings, and more practical, are cotton, linen, wool, leather and synthetic and recycled materials.

Different varieties of blue are found in all these materials, especially those with a French influence. Indeed, France has led the way in textile design since the 17th century, when the French East India Company imported calico and chintz printed with floral and geometric motifs. Known as 'indiennes' after their land of origin, they were hugely popular, and seen as a threat to the well-established silk-weaving industry – so a ban was imposed on the manufacture or sale of all printed cottons in France in 1686.

SEEDS OF INSPIRATION
Salvaged textiles are the starting point
for many decorative schemes – for
example, the 18th-century crewelwork
panel on the bedcover was the inspiration
for this bedroom, and its blue tones
are echoed in the chair upholstery and
blanket (*this page*). Offcuts from larger
projects and pieces of vintage table linen
can be repurposed to make covers for
cushions/pillows and seat pads (*opposite*).

In 1760, after the ban had been lifted, Christophe-Philippe Oberkampf opened a cotton-printing works at Jouy-en-Josas, south-west of Paris, to produce not only indiennes but also toiles de Jouy – cotton fabrics printed with pictorial designs, often of pastoral scenes, flower arrangements or chinoiserie fantasies. Now seen on everything from curtains to quilts, in faded hues of inky grey-blue or rose madder, or in vibrant shades of orange and yellow, toiles de Jouy evoke the essence of a French interior. The indiennes made by Oberkampf, featuring motifs based on traditional Indian and Eastern designs, also remain popular, with new interpretations combining geometric and floral elements.

Many other historical influences are still current today, such as the Victorian legacy of William Morris and the Art Nouveau designers, whose work is known for its birds and animals in foliage, wreathed grapes and vine leaves, along with the more obvious florals.

One joy of living with textiles is making them work together, their different weights, colours, patterns and textures creating a harmonious mix. Natural materials such as cottons and linens, dyed in subtle organic shades taken from nature, nearly always look great together, and are invariably enlivened by an injection of colour from the endlessly versatile blue spectrum.

A MIX OF CONTRASTS
Fabric blues range from the pale watery hue of vintage embroidered linens through the intense indigo of a patchwork tablecloth to the dark navy of striped ticking cushions/pillows (*opposite & this page*). Contrasting shades mix surprisingly well.

PEACE AT THE WATER'S EDGE

Everything about the decorative scheme in this Long Island vacation home spells tranquillity and understatement, creating a perfect backdrop for the eclectic choice of furnishings. The effect of combining pale sky blues with invigorating whites, both inside and out, is to convey a sense of weightlessness, as if the whole structure could simply float away – an effect that is enhanced by the abundance of light that floods in through the windows.

'The light here takes my breath away,' says the owner, Elena Colombo. 'It is an essential feature of the place.' Elena is a sculptor and architectural designer who works in steel, bronze, stone, concrete and bone. She fully appreciates the aesthetic qualities of her cottage at Greenport, on the north fork of Long Island, which she acquired in 2000 as part of a cooperative buyout. It is one of a group of houses surrounded by 36 hectares/ 90 acres of commonly owned land, including a community garden.

The homes were built in the early 20th century to house employees of the Sage Brick Co., which closed after the Great New England Hurricane of 1938. Later, they were rented out as summer cabins, while the brick works itself was replaced by a marina, but for long afterwards bricks continued to be washed ashore. 'We used

CHANGING PERCEPTIONS
The blue-painted floor that graces the entire downstairs of the house appears to change its depth of colour from room to room, depending how the light falls. It is often paired with patterned upholstery in paler shades of blue (*opposite*). Books, glass bottles and display items are also used to echo the overall blue theme (*this page*).

them to make terraces and walkways – so, in theory, the brick works are still with us,' says Elena, who has a deep and abiding love of the place.

This habit of incorporating the old into the new is evident in every facet of Elena's home, which she modernized in stages. Her first priority was to install a cedar-shingle roof, but six layers of asphalt had to be removed before work could begin. The builders discovered that the old roofing boards were still in place, so these were retained and a new roof was laid in accordance with the original pattern.

The interior, whose layout remained largely unchanged, is furnished throughout with pieces from junk shops and the popular local 'dump' – a place where you can leave or take away whatever you like. 'I am always finding real treasures there,' says Elena. 'In fact, I'm convinced that I am blessed with what I call "dump luck".'

The subtlety and simplicity of the blue-and-white colour palette, used on walls, floors and ceilings, make it possible to bring together in each room a cornucopia of disparate items without creating an

ECLECTIC LOOK

Elena's style is to keep the backdrop soft and neutral, and to add bursts of colour in the shape of cushions, throws and accessories. When renovating the interior, she began by choosing a palette of coastal-inspired colours from Farrow & Ball. The living-room walls are a tranquil greyish blue (*above & opposite*), inspired by overcast days when the water and sky seem to blend into one. The mid-century daybed (*above*) was left by the previous owners; Elena reupholstered its full-length seat pad with deckchair stripes and adorned it with cushions/pillows in contrasting and complementary coastal prints. She loves the simplicity of mid-century style, but generally buys things she likes with little or no planning, creating a wonderfully eclectic look.

impression of disunity. In the downstairs living area, there are books of all shapes and sizes, some stacked in piles almost to the ceiling. Other books are arranged haphazardly on white-painted shelves fixed to a section of the ubiquitous sky-blue wall; a collection of empty glass bottles catches the light and adds interest to the display.

Tables, chairs, sofas and sideboards from various periods, and in a variety of woods, some of them painted, coexist in apparent harmony. All these objects have been reclaimed from a previous life elsewhere, each contributing to the overall vintage look, which has been given a fresh twist by the clever use of predominantly white fabrics. Brightly patterned antique rugs enliven the blue-painted floorboards and introduce elements of warmth.

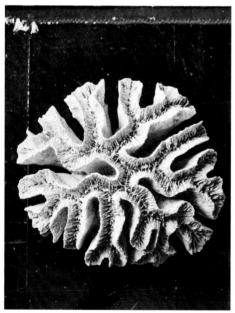

MAKING A SPLASH

When the kitchen and the porch beyond (*opposite & top*) were redecorated in 2017, Elena chose turquoise and marine blue as the main colours, with the vibrant lampshade in the porch becoming a dominant feature. Panelled walls and ceiling were painted brilliant white to match the old farmhouse table and kitchen cabinets. Elena prides herself on using found objects to display in her home. Beautiful coral (*above*), shells, pebbles and driftwood are picked up during walks on the beach; other items come from local thrift stores.

VIEWING SPOTS

At the back of the house, by the water's edge, Elena has installed one of the gas-fuelled fire pits made by her own company, Fire Features (*this page*). Benches and chairs here and in the porch (*opposite*) have been given blue-patterned and blue-striped cushions/pillows, so that everyone can enjoy the spectacular sea views in comfort.

Delft Tiles

The practice of combining blue and white in wall tiles and mosaics goes back to ancient Greece and Rome, and wonderful examples survive in medieval Islamic buildings. Yet modern interpretations can be as innovative as the designs made by Dutch potters in Delft must have seemed in the mid 17th century.

Delftware's white tin-glazed tiles with hand-painted blue patterns were at first produced to imitate porcelain designs imported from China. Images of windmills, small buildings, ships, birds and flowers were soon incorporated, along with scenes from religion and mythology.

The hugely popular Delft tiles were exported throughout Europe, often to be used in fireplaces and in smoky rooms where they could be easily cleaned. In Britain, the technique of transfer printing, developed in the 18th century, allowed such tiles to be mass-produced.

The production of British Delftware declined during the Industrial Revolution, but its artisanal spirit was kept alive by adherents of the Arts and Crafts movement, who favoured both geometrical patterns and floral and animal motifs. Tiles ornamented with plants such as the lily appeared on fireplaces and sideboards, as well as on walls in pantries and kitchens.

In the 21st century, with the resurgence of interest in traditional crafts, Delftware has inspired new interpretations of vintage designs.

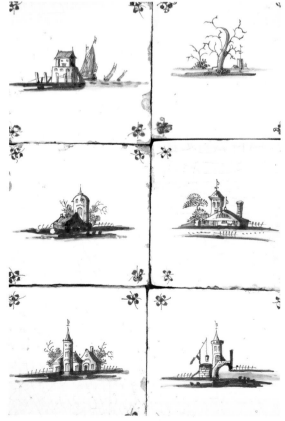

BOLD IDEAS

Delft tiles – both those made to the original designs and more recent imitations – can enhance the character of every room in the home (*this page & opposite*). Often installed in bathrooms and kitchens to protect walls from water damage, they can also be used to introduce decorative interest to living rooms and bedrooms – even, in the boldest examples, to cover an entire wall.

Glassware

Iridescent blue glassware has the power to transform a simple table setting into a veritable work of art.

The effect is particularly rewarding when blue glass is paired with a classic white linen tablecloth or lace-fringed table runner, or arranged on an unadorned surface of oak or pine and complemented by blue-and-white ceramics, napkins and coasters.

Additionally, vintage glass vases, bottles and other containers can be grouped together to make a beautiful display. Hand-blown glass items, if you can find them, are generally far superior in quality to those that are machine-made because the glass is always slightly uneven, so that no piece is exactly the same as any other.

The popularity of blue glass dates from the late 18th century, when the English port of Bristol grew into one of the most important glass-making centres in Europe. It became known for domestic objects – jugs/pitchers, plates, vases, drinking vessels and more – made from adding cobalt oxide to lead crystal to produce a remarkable depth of colour. The city's industry gave rise to many imitators around the world. After a break of 60 years, the manufacture of Bristol Blue glass resumed in the 1980s.

VERSATILE VESSELS

Blue glass, or clear glass with blue decoration, can act as the anchor for a dramatic tablescape. Medicine bottles, vases and other vintage vessels of different shapes and sizes look great when they are arranged on a shelf or table (*this page & opposite*). Some of the original containers were designed to hold poison, with 'Not To Be Taken' stamped on the side.

Every country kitchen needs a big wooden table. Crisp white tablecloths and plenty of blue-and-white china help to set the scene (*this page & opposite*). What makes this room distinctive is the spectacular display of plates around the range cooker and the array of blue glass bottles.

FEAST FOR THE EYES

A working farmhouse for much of its history, this charming home in rural Suffolk needed total restoration and renovation when the current owner moved in 30 years ago with her family. As the oldest parts of the building date from the 16th century, it was decided to make minimal changes to the exterior.

The one diversion from the rule was to build a single-storey addition to the back of the house to allow more light to flood into what would become the kitchen and dining area. New kitchen cabinets and appliances were installed, and an old fireplace was opened up and enlarged to make room for a traditional range cooker.

Elsewhere, the existing internal space was reconfigured to accommodate six bedrooms and several bathrooms. 'It was designed very much as a family home,' says the owner. 'The large garden

and the gently rolling countryside, which is typical of this part of eastern England, were among the big attractions. And there are glorious walks in every direction.' The property is located in a quiet village, but almost entirely surrounded by pasture and agricultural land.

The owner admits to an abiding love for blue and white, and the collections she has accumulated in her home over the years have been founded on that passion. Some of the pieces were inherited and others were given as gifts by friends and family, but most of them were picked up at bric-a-brac shops and antiques markets during travels around England. Rooms throughout the house have been decorated in neutral colours so that the collections can be shown off to best advantage. Much of the wooden furniture is painted white.

Particularly striking is the abundance of blue-and-white plates hung on all three walls in the fireplace recess, behind the cooker, where the brickwork has been left exposed, forming a textural background to the display. The plates themselves are a mix of new and antique, including some with the distinctive willow-pattern design.

On a raised shelf beside the fireplace is an eye-catching arrangement of blue glass bottles of all shapes and sizes, some of them old medicine bottles. A few of the smaller items were found buried in the garden of the old farmhouse when it

AQUA SPLASHES
The floral pattern of the curtains framing the arched window in the kitchen (*opposite*) is a modern take on a vintage design. The dresser/hutch in the dining room includes a number of antique jugs/pitchers in the same colours as the Poole Pottery china and the candles on the table (*this page*). The coordinating splashes of aquamarine look particularly effective when set against the background of white walls and a white linen tablecloth. Napkins and other accessories follow the blue-and-white theme.

NATURE'S PLEASURES
When reupholstering a classic armchair, a modern blue-and-white stripe has been been combined with two contrasting vintage fabrics, both former tablecloths. In proper country syle, the blue grid pattern on the back frames a naturalistic floral design in pinks and greens.

was excavated by the current owners in preparation for replanting; they would form the basis of a much more extensive collection.

In the dining room, which also has exposed brickwork, the plates, cups and saucers were made at Poole Pottery in south-west England between 1958 and 1981. Although produced in enormous quantities, the two-colour Twintone tableware is hard to find today, but can still be picked up in charity sales and on internet sites. Poole Pottery is now a brand name for products made in Stoke-on-Trent in Staffordshire.

Fabrics also exhibit a happy combination of old and new, with traditional florals and narrow-striped ticking predominating. Some genuinely vintage examples are juxtaposed with modern copies of old designs. Blue-and-white checks and wider stripes have been chosen for the curtains and furniture covers in the living room.

BEAUTY IN DIVERSITY
Country-style fabrics such as ginghams and striped and checked linens make good slipcovers for sofas and chairs, and may be mixed and matched without too much regard for coordination. The blend of different furniture styles and fabrics in this living room (*top*) – where a variety of patterns containing different tones of blue have been brought together – creates a relaxed feel. Displayed on the shelves are items from two diverse collections: paintings of domestic subjects interspersed with hand-turned wooden containers (*above*).

The neutral schemes that prevail in the bedrooms mean that these spaces rely for decorative interest on the blue-and-white patterned fabrics used on the beds and hanging at the windows, which include a range of flamboyant florals.

Bathrooms, too, are mostly white-painted and white-tiled, making them easy to clean but potentially rather cold and stark, so a variety of softly draped fabrics has been used to introduce an element of comfort. In one shower room, a length of linen with widely spaced dark-blue stripes has been attached to a standard white shower curtain using pegs/clothespins and left to drape on the floor, while a waterproof curtain concealed behind it keeps the water in the shower tray.

CLASSIC FLORALS

Similar but different interpretations of the rose motif – a classic design element that usually works well with stripes – adorn the nostalgically inspired blue-and-white bed linen in two guest bedrooms (*opposite*). The flamboyant floral fabric and white-painted iron bedstead with rose roundels enliven an otherwise neutral decorative scheme. A trio of blue-bottomed ceramic jugs/pitchers from the 1930s, their necks garlanded with strings of tiny red roses, adds interest to the alcove where a small washbasin and cabinet have been installed (*left*). The bathrooms are mainly white with dashes of blue in towels and shower curtains (*above*). In one room, displayed on a wooden towel rail, is a hand-embroidered cloth decorated with lazy-daisy and stem-stitch flowers (*above left*).

A DASH OF GLAMOUR

A freestanding claw-foot bathtub is the last word in classic design and will add glamour to even the simplest bathroom (*this page*). As the only blue item in the room, it occupies centre stage. To bring dashes of blue into your bathing space, paint one wall or half-wall in the shade of your choice or accessorize with striped towels (*opposite*).

Bathrooms

Its association with water and cleansing makes blue an ideal colour choice for bathrooms, whether it is used in floors or tiles, to paint walls or for accessorizing a white room.

Unless you live in a hot climate, however, take care to avoid a blue that's too cool, which can make the room seem chillier than it would otherwise be.

Cool blues, which often contain an element of ice grey, are among the most sophisticated tones in the colour spectrum, and are now generally associated with Scandinavian interior style. They are soothing and calm, and make a wonderful background for a whole range of other colours, but they are not always suitable for bathrooms.

Warm blues, on the other hand, have a little pink in them, and can be combined with a soft pink and cream to create a look reminiscent of a summer sunset. At the more intense end of the spectrum are clear, uplifting marine blues, which evoke the azure of the Mediterranean or the sunlit turquoise of the Caribbean.

Although you may dream of recreating in your bathroom the colours that recall happy seaside memories, remember that bright blue is a very dominant colour that will achieve much more impact on a wall than it does on a small swatch card, and can make other colours look dirty or dull. To avoid this effect, and to prevent strong colours fighting with each other, the obvious answer is to pair warm, clear blues with creamy white.

The bathroom is a private place – ideally a haven for self-indulgence and pampering – so you can afford to be daring and extravagant when

EXOTIC TOUCHES

Paint, wallpaper and panelling in ultramarine and other intense blues offer a perfect backdrop to vintage bathroom fixtures, such as an original Victorian washbasin with a blue-and-white-patterned inset bowl (*above, above right & right*). Old Delft tiles and a Mallorcan sunflower-design splashback introduce exotic touches – but nothing seems more exotic than a Moroccan brick bathtub covered inside and out with handmade blue tiles (*far right & opposite*).

considering how to decorate it. This is the one space in the house where you might, for example, paint all the walls, and perhaps the ceiling too, in a deep marine blue. The effect will be to create a cosy, cocooning feel, but it will inevitably make the room seem smaller – an effect that can be partly offset by a careful arrangement of lighting.

A subtler way to incorporate a marine feel in your bathroom colour scheme is by painting exposed woodwork/trim, such as cabinet doors, window frames and mirror surrounds, in the blue or blues of your choice. Wall tiles, either plain or patterned, offer great opportunities for experiment – and the more classic your choice of pattern, the more you will evoke a sense of history in the room. Marble-veined linoleum or slate floor tiles with a blue-grey tinge and an appearance of uneven texture have a similar effect.

An old-fashioned kitchen cupboard with half-glazed doors painted pale turquoise (*left*) is used to show off a fine collection of ceramic jugs/pitchers and bowls, cake stands and Kilner jars. Flowers are a ubiquitous feature of Maria Carr's interiors (*above & opposite*); plants and their containers sometimes provide the only colour in an otherwise white room.

FRENCH STYLE IN CALIFORNIA

This intriguing ranch house in the beautiful Ione Valley of northern California combines the attractions of modern prairie living with the character and homeliness of a Provençal country retreat. Although the house was built less than a decade ago, its period architectural details and vintage furniture give it a much older feel – thanks to the ingenuity of its owner Maria Carr, an antiques aficionado with a passion for French farmhouse style.

The ranch building is a single-storey 'kit house' that was delivered, ready to assemble, on a lorry. Three separate kits were joined together to make plenty of space for Maria, her husband and five children. A wood-burning stove and a traditional fireplace were installed, ornate mouldings were added to the window surrounds, and reclaimed 100-year-old tin tiles were attached to the walls of the living room. 'I've always dreamed of living in an older house,' says Maria. 'This one is brand new, but we tried to give it personality.'

As they were busy raising horses and cows on the ranch, the family needed a low-maintenance home, so Maria chose laminate flooring that was simple to clean, and dressed the furniture in white linen slipcovers that could easily be changed and washed.

ACCENTS OF BLUE AND GREEN

In the traditional dining room (*below*), simple bistro chairs, a farmhouse table and curtain rods made from tree branches are combined with a flamboyant teardrop chandelier and gossamer-thin muslin curtains to complete the vintage look. Chairs, stools, bowls, glasses and a huge mirror frame introduce accents of blue and green into the open-plan space – a decorative approach enhanced by the abundance of hydrangea blooms in Maria's preferred colour, a light mauve shading to pale violet blue (*right*).

A cobalt-coloured tin bucket bursting with fragrant lavender makes a good partner for the battered turquoise stool (*left*). Together they add a brilliant splash of colour to the otherwise mainly white scheme in this apparently long-established prairie home. In reality, the house was built less than a decade ago, but it has been given the patina of age by the addition of features such as ornate mouldings around the windows. In the living room (*below*), a cast-iron wood-burning stove and traditional fireplace were installed, and reclaimed tin tiles were attached to the walls and painted white. Sofas with white slipcovers are piled high with plump cushions/pillows made from vintage ticking.

Only late in the day did Maria introduce coloured elements into the decorative scheme, having initially favoured an all-white palette. 'I was a bit afraid of adding colour,' she admits. 'When we moved in, I painted all the walls pure, brilliant white – but because of the huge windows, it was harsh and a bit cold. It felt as though something was missing.'

The solution was to repaint the interior walls in a soft putty grey, creating a much warmer effect: 'I bought a pale blue wardrobe/armoire for our dining area and it looked so lovely that I soon got over my phobia of colour.'

She loves the impact of blue accents against an all-white or off-white background. 'I moved over 25 times in my lifetime and one of my favourite places was on a ranch by the ocean in southern California,' says Maria. 'A pop of blue in a room takes me back to my time there.'

Maria makes twice-yearly trips to France, where she scours markets and brocantes for characterful items, especially those once used for agricultural purposes. She loves handmade antiques, vintage linens and faded, rough-textured wooden

furniture that has seen better days. Simplicity is her guiding light, but she likes to add unexpected touches to an interior, such as pairing a crystal chandelier with a salvaged farmhouse table: 'These disparate objects go together in a way that stops a room seeming too fancy or overdecorated.' She also has a self-confessed obsession with doors, especially those made from faded, aged wood that has lost its natural grain. By easy tricks such as leaning old wooden shutters against a bedroom wall, Maria has succeeded in giving her American home an authentic French flavour.

Maria now shares her knowledge and inspiration with others by writing an antiques blog, Dreamy Whites, which has in turn led to the setting up of a successful retail venture. 'When people following the blog started to ask me where I bought the things in my home, I thought I might as well start selling them,' she says, 'so my blog inspired my online shop.'

ARTISTIC ARRANGEMENTS
Maria's early hopes of becoming a painter were overtaken by family commitments, but her artistic talents are evident everywhere in the treatment of reclaimed and recycled treasures (*this page & opposite*). Ceramic pots and jugs/pitchers, plastic moulds, rolls of old fabric and Provençal shopping baskets are arranged inside distressed wooden cupboards; a collection of greenish-blue glass 'bubbles' are displayed decoratively in a wire fisherman's basket; and turquoise-painted wooden doors and shutters are propped up against pale-grey walls.

EVOKING NOSTALGIA
Their resilience means that enamel pieces are often passed down through the generations, surviving for decades. Items such as old teapots, coffee-pots, storage jars and jugs/pitchers and bowls that were originally used for washing are both practical and decorative (*this page & opposite*). Retro modern versions are also in demand, especially in the kitchen, where enamelware is always at home.

Enamelware

Enamel dishes and storage jars were a common feature in kitchens of the 1930s and 1940s, while shiny white enamel plates and mugs with a thin blue-black rim evoke nostalgic memories of picnics and alfresco dining in the 1960s.

Enamelware went out of fashion in the latter part of the 20th century, but it has had a tremendous revival in recent years, and some vintage pieces have become highly collectible.

The enamelling process involves smelting finely ground glass into a liquid, applying it to a metal base and baking it at high temperatures to create a smooth vitreous coating. There may be several layers – an undercoat, a base coat and a colour or colours – and each is dried before the next is applied.

It is the combination of glass and metal that makes enamelware virtually unbreakable, though it is vulnerable to chipping. Chips cannot be repaired, but small imperfections may add to an item's charm. Enamel objects are coloured by adding various minerals such as cobalt and iron, and they may be illustrated by hand using the sgraffito technique. Particularly beautiful effects are seen in swirl and speckled enamelware.

Enamel is now used to make a huge range of items – from teapots and mugs to bread bins/breadboxes, plates and wall tiles. As well as being easy to clean, enamel cooking pots are heat-resistant and can be used on the hob/stovetop and in the oven. Look out also for vintage enamel jugs/pitchers, which were used for carrying hot water in the days before modern plumbing.

Lighting

Lighting comes in many forms and serves several different purposes.

Combining well-placed table lamps with soft ceiling spotlights, for example, will dictate the mood of a room. Lights, like colours, have the power to make a room seem bigger or smaller, warmer or cooler. Adequate task lighting is vital in a home office, a kitchen or a reading space.

Precisely directed lighting that is used to draw the eye to a beautiful object is usually described as feature lighting. But a light fixture can be a feature in itself – and that is the type of lighting that takes centre stage when decorating with blue and white.

As well as performing a useful function, all the light fixtures shown here have been chosen by the homeowners to make statements – some more dramatic than others, especially in the case of pendant lights and vintage designs. Even the simplest of white-painted rooms can be given a touch of glamour by the addition of a flamboyant chandelier, while a blue-tinged wall wall sconce can be used to ground a swirly blue-patterned wallpaper. At the more utilitarian end of the spectrum are white or tinted metal desk lamps and chunky lanterns, adding a modern touch to otherwise traditional settings.

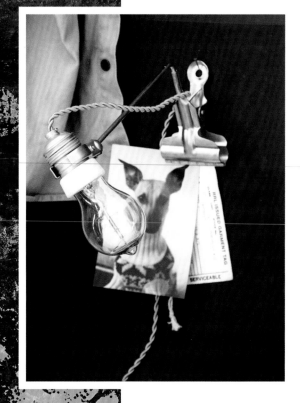

MAKING AN IMPACT
Neutral schemes are brought to life by well-chosen feature lighting (*this page & opposite*). An elaborate chandelier with a mass of blue droplets or a pair of turquoise lantern-shaped pendants will add drama to a dining area. Even a simple paper globe, a Victorian-style lamp fitting with a patterned 'petticoat' or a naked bulb attached to a blue metal hinge can make a real impact.

A PLACE TO RELAX

Lining the terrace are plenty of teak sunbeds with white seat covers (*left*), their comfortably raked backs and footrests inviting guests to indulge in an afternoon snooze. Lifebelts displaying the name of the house (*above*) are decorative rather than functional. The blue-and-white geometric pattern on the beach towels reflects the decorative theme adopted throughout the house.

BRETON INSPIRATIONS

The imposing exterior of this traditional Breton house, with its steeply pitched slate roof, tall chimneys and narrow shuttered windows, offers no hint of the decorative surprise awaiting those people who are lucky enough to cross the threshold – for almost every room contains a dramatic feast of blues, carefully crafted by its owners, Laurence and Yves Sabouret.

Dating from the early 20th century, the creeper-clad house, surrounded by dense vegetation, crowns a rocky promontory outside the walled city of St Malo. It conforms to a style of architecture found all over this part of Brittany, described by Laurence as 'inherited from the Normandy example seen at Deauville, but with a typical Breton twist'. In the main living room, the walls are covered with traditional oak boiseries, and there is a large fireplace, also in oak, carved with Breton motifs. Most of the windows in the house have sturdy louvred shutters,

EN PLEIN AIR

A shaded terrace high above the sea is the perfect place for an alfresco summer lunch (*above*). Its white-painted floor and railings evoke an atmosphere of the tropics. The variety of blues in the china, glass and cutlery/flatware echoes the interior colour scheme, while a red-and-white tablecloth adds zest to the occasion. Framed by dark-needled pines, the view from the terrace is breathtaking (*opposite below*).

which give good protection against wind, cold and excessive heat. Rather than paint over the dark oak panelling and destroy some of the building's character, Laurence has used an abundance of white to lighten the interior, along with many different shades of blue. She favours blues that evoke the Caribbean, the French Riviera and the Greek islands, as well as the paler, more subtle blues of Brittany itself. When the weather is good in Brittany, she says, 'The sea can be like a light-green or blue lagoon. The water is transparent.'

Lazy summer days are spent on the tree-shaded terrace, whose white-painted floor and railings are redolent of the tropics. For the comfort of their guests, the Sabourets have provided plenty of teak-framed deck loungers with off-white

ORIGINAL INTEGRITY
Dark oak panelling, beams and ornate arched doors are prominent features downstairs (*above*). To retain the original integrity of the interior, it was decided not to paint the panels and doors in a lighter colour. Instead, the décor has been updated by the display of objects with maritime associations, and by the injection of blue-and-white pattern in the form of chair covers and tablecloths.

ENTERTAINING IN STYLE
Plates, bowls and other ceramics, many sourced from local markets and brocantes, have often been chosen for their classic blue-and-white patterns (*this page*). The Sabourets are generous hosts, and the constant stream of guests creates plenty of opportunities for the beautiful Breton pottery and napkins to be put to good use – though at other times, glasses, plates and the like may be incorporated into a display. In accordance with the main colour scheme, even the knives and forks have blue handles (*left*).

cotton cushions/pillows, and there is an awning to give extra shade from the sun. The view from here is breathtaking: framed by the branches of pines and the shape of the rocky outcrops is the sea, dotted in summer with scores of boats.

Indoors from the terrace is the main living area, where the luxurious sofas have soft white covers piped in dark blue and arranged around a patterned rug in the same tones. Contrasting with the white covers is a mixture of cushions/pillows, some covered in a plain azure fabric to match the generous curtains, others in a geometrical pattern and yet others in an indienne design.

To these elements have been added white Roman blinds/shades and a white cabriole-legged French table covered with rows of sea-washed shells and a collection of cerulean glass, models and paintings of yachts.

The same colours reappear in the main bedroom, one of the few areas in which pattern has been given a leading role, its most dominant feature being a geometrical wallpaper in blue and white. White curtains and bed linen add a refreshing crispness to the decorative scheme, which includes objects with maritime associations.

Elsewhere in the house, patterned Provençal tablecloths and blue-and-white European and Chinese ceramics are teamed with navigational charts and nautical pictures.

All the interventions made by the Sabourets in the interior of their Brittany home are designed to exploit the spectacular northern light in this part of France, which is more subtle than the bright light of the Mediterranean. Over the years it has attracted a host of artists, including Monet, Boudin, Signac and many lesser-known names.

UNIFYING PALETTE

Covered in creamy-white cotton with dark-blue piping, the sofas in the living room (*left & opposite*) make a refreshing complement to the blue curtains. A palette of brilliant cerulean and sea blues, offset by shades of white, unifies the decorative objects like glass bottles, lamp stands and white decoy birds with practical elements such as rugs, tables and curtains. The collection of shells (*right*) includes examples of limpet, mussel, scallop and cockle shells, found on nearby beaches.

CRESCENDO OF COLOUR

A vibrant geometrical wallpaper in different densities of blue interspersed with small squares of white makes a dramatic impact in the main sleeping space (*right*). Even in this room, however, the basic blues, creams and whites remain in control, with the crisp white curtains and blue-and-white bed linen creating a calming counterpoint to the flamboyant pattern – and the shirt hanging in front of the window is just the right shade of blue. The floor has been painted white to enhance the strong light from the sea.

MARINE MUSE
The steeply sloping slate roofs, tall chimneys and narrow windows are typical of a traditional architectural style associated with this part of the Brittany coast. From the terrace there are spectacular views of the yacht-filled bay, which has been such a vital inspiration to the Sabourets in their choice of interior decoration.

Kitchen cupboards and armoires, along with vintage tabletops and chests of drawers/dressers that have seen better days, are good candidates for a paint job (*right, far right & opposite*). For a Swedish interpretation of 18th-century French furniture, try painting the inside shelves and back of an armoire in a punchy bright blue (*below*).

Furniture Blues

Painted furniture, especially of the weathered and distressed variety, will add character to any room.

You can either pick up ready-painted items from bric-a-brac shops or antiques arcades, or do it yourself by transforming reclaimed dark brown furniture with a few coats of white, cream or blue. The paint could be either matt or gloss, depending on the impression you want to achieve, but matt 'weathers' more effectively. If newly painted furniture looks too fresh and pristine, don't despair; a few years of heavy domestic use will knock it into shape.

In both vintage and modern pieces, different shades of blue are frequently seen. Pale sky blues and greyish blues are particularly well suited to Scandinavian-style decorative schemes and Shaker interiors, both of which are distinguished by their simplicity and clean lines.

These colours, which have a lightening effect on an interior, are commonly used to decorate side tables, chests of drawers/dressers, cabinet doors and even on kitchen dressers/hutches, armoires and painted wooden chairs.

Deeper, darker blues can be very dominant and should be used sparingly in painting large pieces of wooden furniture. They can work well in plain or patterned fabric form, however, when made into fitted chair and sofa covers, or added as accent colours to enliven an otherwise white scheme.

Coastal

The human passion for blue-and-white decoration is often inspired by the colours of the sea, from palest sky blue to deepest indigo, as seen in many coastal homes. Whether you dream of a Mediterranean fisherman's cabin, a luxurious beachside house in South Africa or a relaxed cottage on Long Island, there is something here for you. As well as a focus on outdoor living, there are features on bedrooms, geometric patterns, walls, floors and displaying prized collections.

FRAMING A VIEW

This unassuming beach cabin (*left*) is one of a group of similar whitewashed buildings clustered around a quiet Spanish cove. All the woodwork/trim, inside and out, is painted a vibrant turquoise (*below & opposite*); in spaces such as the dining room, the turquoise shutters are left open to frame a view. Beach finds such as corals (*above*) can provide colour inspiration or be treasured as items for display.

FISHERMAN'S COTTAGE

Just off the coast of Alicante in south-eastern Spain is the tiny island of Portichol, covering an area of little more than 8 hectares/20 acres. Apart from the sea, Portichol is the only physical feature that can be seen from Jessica Bataille's cottage on the mainland – a traditional Spanish fisherman's cabin set in a secluded cove surrounded by rocky cliffs.

The building, dating from the mid 20th century, is one of a cluster of whitewashed cottages overlooking the beach, all of which have shutters, doors and window frames in various shades of blue. Jessica chose a vibrant turquoise for her home, to reinforce its distinctive seaside character. She is an interior designer with her own store in nearby Javea, located on the easternmost point of Spain's Mediterranean coast. The market town's connections with the fishing industry go back to Roman times.

When Jessica and her partner, Ivan, saw the cabin for the first time, its only contents were a jumble of fishing nets and a few basic items of furniture. Before taking up residence, they had to create a kitchen from scratch and to renovate all the other rooms. There was a boat on the roof, which they used for sleeping in while the building works were carried out.

The strict planning laws that apply to coastal properties in Spain meant that a radical renovation was impossible, so Jessica and Ivan decided to restrict their changes to practical interventions that were sympathetic to the building's original purpose and setting. Since the cabin is not connected to the local electricity grid, one of the first things they did was to install solar panels for power generation.

The interior colour scheme was carefully chosen to mirror the colours of the seascape, with white walls and turquoise woodwork/trim. Furniture is plain and functional. Distressed and worn wooden pieces are mixed and matched with rattan stools and chairs and teamed with woven natural-fibre rugs to create a relaxed atmosphere. The rattan lampshades, which recall woven lobster pots, add warmth and texture.

Accessories and furniture were mainly sourced from local flea markets, and from the town of Gata de Gorgos, which has several shops specializing in the wicker furniture typical of this part of the Mediterranean, including ladder-back wooden chairs with wicker seats.

The kitchen features simple whitewashed walls and cabinets, with the turquoise-painted window frame above the sink adding a splash of colour. The robust terracotta tiles in this room can easily be swept clean of sand and stones and mopped down, though Jessica says that, to keep the house in harmony with its surroundings, she would prefer to replace the tiles with a pebble floor. Most of the ceramics, in the kitchen and elsewhere, were made by local artisans.

WHITE ON WHITE
The kitchen is small but perfectly formed (*opposite*). The white-painted cabinets were constructed from bricks and reclaimed wooden doors, while mottled terracotta floor tiles add warmth to the scheme and are easy to keep clean. A handmade shelving unit in the dining space (*above*) is used to display a collection of tableware, which incorporates a variety of blue-and-white patterns and images. All-white mugs, bowls and plates are also in evidence, as is an inclination for layering white on white (*top*).

When it comes to choosing textiles, Jessica is drawn instinctively to washed linen and striped cotton, complemented by splashes of brighter colour and pattern in the form of cushion/pillow covers from her shop in Javea.

Rustic wooden stools and a low rattan table outside the front door provide a perfect spot from which to watch the world go by. Jessica says that her most treasured moments occur here in the early morning, when she is gazing out to sea. The prospect reminds her of a Picasso painting of a girl at the water's edge.

A TREASURED SPOT

Apart from the sea itself and the occasional passing vessel, the only significant landmark visible from the shore is the tiny island of Portichol (*this page*). As elsewhere in the cabin, the living room (*opposite*) features white walls and terracotta floor tiles. Colour accents of turquoise, dark blue and yellow recur throughout, and simple geometric patterns add interest to the scheme.

Outdoor Living

The chance to spend many hours of the day in the open air, enjoying the natural world in all its moods, is one of the great attractions of living in a coastal location.

To some, such an existence may seem as desirable as an endless holiday. You can get up early in the morning and walk along the beach, disturbed only by the call of seabirds in flight or the sight of waders feeding along the shoreline. During the day you can languish in comfortable chairs in your garden or outdoor space, reading, chatting with friends or simply watching the world go by. And at night you can see the sun go down and watch the moon casting a path of spectral light across the waves.

Real life isn't always like that, of course. Your house by the sea may be a place of work as well as a home, or a permanent family residence, in which case the domestic requirements will be quite different from those of a holiday retreat. Coastal homes are often exposed to violent storms and salt-laden winds, so any furniture or other objects left outdoors need to be as sturdy and as weatherproof as possible.

One feature common to almost every coastal home, whatever its main function, is an outside living area, where meals are taken on fine days. An outdoor space must be, above all, practical and comfortable, and decorated with beautiful objects, including beach finds and old storm lanterns. If you can, construct a covered area for shelter against inclement weather, and keep the ambience casual by installing reclaimed garden furniture such as a set of slatted folding chairs and a bare wooden

LAID-BACK LOUNGING
Fabrics in blue and white – whether plain or patterned – are sure to vitalize any outdoor space. Low-level furniture can be piled high with cushions/pillows and soft throws to create an irresistibly comfortable lounging area (*this page & opposite*).

tabletop on metal trestles. Add a white linen tablecloth, blue-and-white china, cutlery/flatware and a set of blue glasses, and you are all set for a relaxed alfresco lunch.

Exterior wooden doors, shutters and window frames in seaside homes are often painted turquoise to harmonize with the setting. Movable pieces such as tables, benches and chairs may get the same treatment. Paints used for this purpose must be highly durable and resistant to peeling and flaking, while allowing the wood to breathe.

Fabrics in blue and white – plain, patterned, striped or checked – enliven any outdoor space, most commonly seen in cushion/pillow covers and pads for chairs and sunloungers. If you want to make the most of sea breezes, hang vibrantly coloured drapes around exposed seating areas to add a touch of exoticism. A checked blue-and-white tablecloth and matching napkins recall happy episodes spent whiling away the hours in cafés on the New England coast or beside the azure Mediterranean.

PATINA OF AGE

In a seaside setting, outdoor tables, seating and even metal storm lanterns painted turquoise or aquamarine look very appealing, especially if they match the exterior doors, shutters and window frames. These painted objects will look even more attractive after a few years of use, when they have acquired a charmingly timeworn appearance (*this page & opposite*).

SAVING SPACE

Hanging pots and pans from butcher's hooks fixed to a wooden beam (*above*) is a great way to save space in a small kitchen. Other ideas include an integral rack for draining and storing plates, and small shelves for containers (*left & below*). The blue-painted wall cupboard has a wire-mesh front for an airier feel. Cooking equipment and kitchen accessories can be found in various shades of blue (*opposite*).

NATURAL SERENITY

Set on the southern tip of the African continent, this exquisite coastal cabin is largely surrounded by 'fynbos', the natural shrubland of the Western Cape and Eastern Cape provinces of South Africa, and the lush vegetation encroaches right up to the outdoor decking. Every element of the house, inside and out, is inspired by its seaside location.

With its white-painted shingles and corrugated-iron roof, the South African house has a distinctive architectural style reminiscent of Cape Cod, Massachusetts. The owners decided that the interior should be kept as minimal and as simple as possible in order to allow the outdoor landscape to take centre stage. For example, the two easy armchairs and oversized footstools that furnish the open-plan downstairs living area are upholstered in a muted sky-blue fabric – soft shades deliberately chosen to blend with the colours of nature. They face outwards at all times, encouraging family and friends to relax and

EXHILARATING BREEZES
Soft sky blue and white is
a classic combination, and
in a white open-plan room
where checks and stripes
provide the only decorative
pattern, the small space looks
airy and expansive, with the
colours accurately reflecting
the natural world outside. The
comfortable chairs are always
turned to face outwards, for
enjoyment of the view. A
polished-concrete floor runs
throughout the lower level,
adding a brilliant gleam.

enjoy glorious views of the ocean and the vegetation, and to watch the activities of the abundant animal life. A silent observer can sometimes see small bush buck and various species of lizard exploring near the deck, and from June to December southern right whales and humpbacks come very close inshore to breed and mate.

The land on which the house stands forms part of South Africa's Cape Floral Region, designated a UNESCO World Heritage Site on account of its exceptional diversity of flora and fauna. More than two-thirds of the 9,000 plant species found in the fynbos are endemic, meaning that they grow naturally nowhere else in the world. There is also a large number of endemic animal and bird species.

The open-plan layout of the cabin keeps the rooms airy and cool whatever the season, even at the height of the sweltering South African summer. With sliding doors wide open to the sea, and the front door propped ajar, fresh sea breezes are allowed to waft through the living room and tiny kitchen throughout the day. Another effective aid to ventilation is the high ceiling in the main part of the building, which reaches right up to roof height. A staircase with open treads leads up from the living area to the sole double bedroom, which is located on a mezzanine level in the apex of the roof.

A freestanding unit with a hob/stovetop built into the work surface separates the kitchen from the main living area. This is an imaginative solution to dividing up the space economically, without the need to build interior walls. It has the added advantage of allowing whoever is doing the cooking to appreciate the view through the open glass doors.

Easy to sweep clean and wash, the polished-concrete floor adds an overall gleam to the lower storey of the house, which is softened and made cosier by the earth-coloured woollen rugs under the chairs.

Exposed ceiling joists, stairs and walls are all painted brilliant white, a feature that adds to the sense of space

EYE-CATCHING ACCESSORIES
Furniture in the dining area consists of a scrubbed wooden table and teak folding chairs (*opposite*), while in the corner stands an antique storage cupboard with a weathered appearance. Complementing the simple furnishings are several eye-catching accessories. The table has been set for supper with china in two shades of blue, for example; in place of a napkin or a place name, each guest is greeted by a washed pebble and a sliver of driftwood (*above left*). An ornate cast-iron candelabra on the side cabinet adds a touch of glamour (*above centre*), and a blue enamel container is used to display a collection of beach finds (*above right*).

and coolness, and brings together all the different elements of the structure. The only colour is seen in the blue stripes and checks of the upholstery and cushions/pillows, and the splashes of blue on the kitchen cabinet doors and in culinary accessories. A unified theme of blue and white means you can mix large and small checks together with a variety of stripes when you layer up cushions/pillows on a chair or sofa.

The house is newly built, but traditional tongue-and-groove boards have been fitted all the way around the lower half of each room and painted white. The simplicity of the interior style, with its compact, boat-like arrangement of facilities, again recalls the beach houses of Cape Cod, with their seafaring heritage and decorative tradition of blue-and-white stripes.

SNOWY SCENE
A sleigh bed is adorned with snowy cotton bed linen. Four shades of blue – duck egg, aqua, teal and petrol – make up the pattern embroidered on the pillowcases and duvet/comforter cover. A spray of blue delphiniums in a vase completes the scene.

The white bathroom has been given interest and texture by the installation of a bathtub panel and splashback made from watery-blue glass mosaic tiles. The tiles are functional and aesthetically pleasing, protecting the walls and bathtub panel from water damage, and introducing a beautifully iridescent surface as a visual counterpoint to the white walls. Similarly, in the bedroom, accents of blue are used to soften the rather stark effect of an otherwise all-white scheme.

BRINGING THE OUTSIDE IN

The angular lines of the deep bathtub and shelf unit are echoed in the strips of sky-blue mosaic tiles lining the walls (*right*), but the effect is softened by piles of textiles and the rounded shapes of sea urchin shells. A cast-iron peg rail for bathrobes (*above*) signals that the beach is just outside the door. Plain and spotted towels are teamed with a striped rag-rug bathmat, all in contrasting shades of blue (*top*).

Bedrooms

A bedroom is a private place in which you can be free to express your personal taste, whether it tends towards simplicity, tradition or flamboyance.

Historically, whites and creams, pastels and neutrals have been the favourite choice for bedrooms. Regarded as soothing and sleep-inducing, these colours still have an important role in sleeping spaces – there is nothing more appealing than crisp white linen sheets, freshly laundered – but adding elements of strong colour can enhance the character of a room.

From the palest aquamarine to the deepest indigo, the wide spectrum of blues presents endless possibilities for coastal-style decoration in bedrooms. When combined with creamy white or oyster grey in stripes and other geometric patterns, the blue cornucopia becomes even richer.

Blue-and-white patterns incorporating nautical motifs such as boats, seagulls and beach scenes are another variation on the theme. If you live by water, there is no better way to bring the outside in than through the combination of blue and white.

The softness and texture of fabrics are essential to the comfort of a bedroom. Their colours and patterns will complement the hard surfaces and straight lines of the bed, hanging cupboards and chests of drawers/ dressers, and create focal points within the room.

Vibrant marine blues make a great impact in plain or patterned curtains and window blinds/shades, and in duvet/comforter covers, chair seats and bedspreads. Blues of every variety can been seen in those most desirable objects: American patchwork quilts and traditional French quilts known as *boutis*. Often graced with floral patterns, *boutis* and other quilts are widely used on both sides of the Atlantic as bed coverings, throws and even sometimes tablecloths.

SOPHISTICATED SCHEMES
When teamed with white, neutral or cream walls, doors and ceilings, narrow stripes and small checks make a good foundation for a sophisticated bedroom scheme, with touches of darker hues or a splash of bold pattern for drama (*this page & opposite*).

The centrepiece of a bedroom is the bed itself, so its appearance needs to be given plenty of thought. The quickest and easiest way to put together a gorgeous-looking bed is to use plain white or off-white sheets, pillowcases and duvet/comforter, and add one sumptious bed covering, which could be a blanket, eiderdown or quilt. For further sophistication, add another bed covering and a few throws and start experimenting with different combinations, some spread out over the bed, some folded and others hung artfully over the foot.

If you are feeling more adventurous, opt for pale or dark blue bed linen and adorn the bed with a mixture of pillows and cushions with covers in contrasting prints. Pair different shades, periods and fabric textures, or juxtapose stripes with graphic designs.

RELAXED VIBES

Soft aquamarine and pale turquoise dominate the cooling colour scheme in these relaxed bedrooms by the sea (*opposite, above & right*). In a Spanish coastal home, painted shutters add extra aqua accents to both the inside and outside of the house (*above right*). By contrast, a dark blue patterned blind/shade makes a fierce statement in a room where everything is painted bright white (*far right*).

SOFT AND VIBRANT
Above the fireplace in the living room is a painting by Jennifer Ebner, a Connecticut artist, the lower third of which consists of a wide blue horizontal stripe (*opposite*). It represents everything the owners wanted the house to be: 'abstract and modern, but totally organic and natural'. The subtle use of both soft and vibrant blues in fabrics, furnishings and displays reflects this vision (*left, above & below*).

HISTORY RECAPTURED

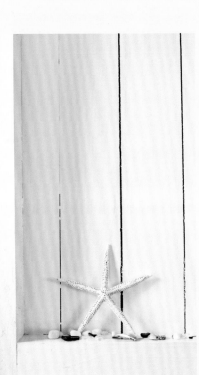

This beguiling summer retreat on Long Island Sound – which was once two separate cottages – didn't always have such a bright and airy look. Built without foundations, it was standing directly on the earth and gradually rotting away. What's more, one earlier resident had had the property 'winterized' so that it could be lived in all year round, with the result that the interior had become dark and damp.

When the current owners bought the house in 2012, they hired architect John Allee and interior designer Hannah Childs to restore it to its former glory. Inspiration came from the entrance hall, which was built when the two cottages were joined together in the late 19th century. Some original elements had survived in the space – exposed beams, timber-framed walls, sash windows and wooden floors – and it was these features that provided the model for a wholesale renovation.

INSPIRATIONS FROM THE PAST

It was the hallway (*opposite*), built when the two original cottages were joined together, that inspired the purchase of the cottage. The owners loved the exposed wooden framing and used it as a model for the entire renovation. The blue-painted bench was the first piece of furniture they acquired. In the dining room (*this page*), the mandala-patterned rug, the linen tablecloth and napkins, and the striped seat covers are coordinated in similar shades of washed-out blue. Leading up from the dining room is a boxed-in staircase where a sturdy old mooring rope is used instead of a handrail.

The first stage was to raise the whole building by 1.8m/6ft in order to lay a reinforced-concrete base. Remarkably, it was lifted and lowered back onto the new foundations by mechanical means. The exterior walls were clad in white cedar shingles typical of New England coastal architecture, which turn silvery grey as they weather.

False ceilings and walls were removed to expose the building's original structural framework, and a new kitchen and new bathrooms were installed. According to Hannah, the owners favoured a very simple, clean aesthetic, so the entire interior was painted in Benjamin Moore's White Dove. They also wanted the cottage to feel lived in, with a relaxed mix of old and new. New floors of reclaimed pine were laid downstairs, while existing pine floors on the upper level were sanded and varnished to bring out the warm tones of the wood. Kitchen cabinets and countertops were handcrafted by a local carpenter and old chestnut floorboards were repurposed as shelves. An antique farmhouse table was paired with white metal Tolix chairs.

Wherever colour is to be found, it has almost always been chosen from the blue spectrum – and set against a background of white and neutrals, the blue invariably makes a strong impact. An arresting feature of the kitchen, for example, is a painted navy-blue stripe, reminiscent of old French linen, running down the centre of the staircase.

The living-room décor is a mixture of rustic and modern. Neutral linens were chosen for the sofa and armchairs, with touches of subtle blues and greens in the shape of cushions/ pillows and throws. In the bedrooms and bathrooms, too, various different blues are incorporated in striped quilts, floral bed linen and geometric-patterned rugs. 'The palette of whites, blues and neutrals [chosen by the owners] has opened my eyes to new challenges and solutions,' says Hannah, 'while renewing my appreciation of simplicity.'

CALMING HAVENS
Vintage linens were the inspiration for the painted staircase that leads off the kitchen, and the handrail was crafted from a length of old copper piping (*top*). Walls throughout the house have been whitewashed to keep the look cohesive and to show off the original panelling; this theme is continued into the bathroom (*above*), where a striped navy-blue-and-white rug injects a vibrant note. The bedrooms are calming havens of soft pastel blues, greys and greens, with woven fabrics contributing textural interest (*opposite*).

A SERENE SCENE

The exterior of this seaside cottage is clad in cedar shingles that are typical of the local area and will gradually weather to a beautiful silvery grey. The deck furniture has a muted colour palette, apart from the chic piping around the seat covers and the abstract pattern of the cushions/pillows, incorporating a dark indigo.

Pattern

Stripes, checks, zigzags and geometric patterns can be a welcome antidote to an overdose of floral nostalgia, but it needn't be a choice of one or the other.

The two design styles can work remarkably well together, especially when coordinated by a matching or complementary shade of blue. Indeed, a coordinating blue can make it possible to mix a surprising diversity of florals and stripes, or stripes and geometrics.

A private space such as a bedroom, where you can be free to express your personality, is the ideal place to experiment with a multitude of patterns. You may feel tempted to try out one of the large floral or wheel-shaped designs that are now popular, or spice up an otherwise plain scheme with a zingy chevron rug.

Perennially popular for any room in the house are the two types of stripe that predominate in French-influenced fabric design: traditional cotton ticking, originally confined to blue and grey, but now available in several modern variations; and a design incorporating stripes of different widths often seen in subtle combinations of blue, beige, pink and cream.

MODERN RETRO

Inspired by 1950s and 1960s style, the company Mini Moderns has designed dazzling geometric patterns for bed coverings and wallpaper, including Backgammon, based on the game's discs and triangles (*left, right & opposite*). French ticking and an Indian-inspired Provençal fabric (*above right & far right*) offer more familiar geometric alternatives.

Some floor rugs in chevron and other vibrant patterns are now made from recycled plastic bottles, which makes them easy to clean as well as eco-friendly. Although the hunt is on among manufacturers to find sustainable fabrics for clothing and furniture that degrade easily, there are many problems to overcome in the production process, so the increased use of recycled materials is currently the best way to avoid adding to global pollution.

DEEPEST BLUE

Traditional furniture can be upholstered in anything from classic chinz or damask to cotton fabrics with swirling abstract patterns or pinstripes. What unites all the disparate textiles seen here is the deepest of deep indigo blues (*this page & opposite*).

WHITE SPACE OPENING UP TO THE SEA

Grotto Bay, on the south-west coast of South Africa, not far from Cape Town, is the site of this spectacular beachside house. Its bedroom doors fold back on two sides of the building to reveal views of verdant hills, sweeping sand dunes and crashing surf. Water from a shallow pool laps the concrete terrace, and there is a deeper plunge pool for anyone in search of a refreshing dip.

The house is orientated to take full advantage of the surrounding landscape, and many of the rooms open out onto their own area of private deck. In the main bedroom, as in the rest of the house, colour has been kept to a minimum; in this case, a plain cotton duvet/comforter cover in soft aquamarine and a pair of toning pillowcases represent everything that's needed to bring a suggestion of the sea indoors.

A desire for simplicity and lack of ostentation inspired the choice of furniture. The base of the four-poster bed, for example, was made from reclaimed wooden posts, still with lingering vestiges of paint, and given a similarly unadorned frame that looks perfectly at home in the high-ceilinged room. There is no need for fabric bed hangings, since these would impede the flow of cooling breezes on hot, airless nights. The oval stone-composite bathtub – a luxurious addition to the sleeping space – is raised on a dais so that bathers can soak up the wonderful views.

STARFISH GARLANDS

Although the interior spaces in this beachside home have an aura of simple luxury, some of the furniture pieces have been made from very modest materials. Reclaimed wooden posts were used to form a base and frame for the four-poster bed, whose only decoration is a pair of white starfish garlands.

If you favour a classic all-white interior, as shown here, it is important to take account of the type of climate and quality of natural light that you are dealing with, and to bear in mind that cool off-whites, which include a dash of blue or black, produce a very different effect from warm whites. The choice of pure white works really well only in those countries where strong sunlight and deep shadows are apparent every day; in such settings, a brilliant white room can feel appealingly cool and serene. In colder northern realms, where sunlight is less frequent and the light itself is less intense, white often looks better and less stark when combined with a little yellow or grey. Warmer-toned whites, such as ivory, buttermilk, barley white and pale cream, are soft and calming and associated with luxury.

A white or off-white room has the advantage of allowing furnishings to speak for themselves without having to compete with strong colours or patterns on the walls. Whatever the shade of white you choose, a room painted in such simple fashion becomes a bare canvas that can be dressed to reflect many different moods.

The house at Grotto Bay has eight sleeping spaces of various shapes and sizes, including a tiny bedroom in the attic. All the bedrooms are painted white, and all are decorated with features that reflect the seaside location. There is also a spacious dining room whose main elements could be described as simplicity itself – apart from an enormous glass chandelier, which adds a theatrical flourish. The tongue-and-groove panelled walls are painted white; bare floorboards are stained with a pale chalky white; and the furniture is understated and timeless. The inclusion of natural elements, such as seagrass chair seats and a rattan easy chair, ensures that the room reflects the changing tones of nature, with texture as the dominant factor, and its daytime look is fresh and elegant.

INDONESIAN INDIGO
The most prominent feature of this cosy bedroom in the attic (*above*) is the intense indigo of its Indonesian-style bed linen. The stone-composite bathtub in the main bedroom (*opposite*) is set on a dais so that bathers can appreciate the coastal views.

ALFRESCO SHOWER

In a secluded corner, reclaimed and weather-worn timber has been used for a rustic-looking outdoor shower screen (*above & right*). A decorative garland, hung from a nail in the screen, brightens up the greyish-brown wood with touches of blue and white; lengths of jute string have been threaded with shells, blue glass and white ceramic beads, and tied onto a metal ring covered in raffia.

SUN, SEA AND SKY

This wooden beach house has a steeply pitched corrugated-iron roof and wide overhang, which, like the rest of the building, are painted white (*left & opposite*). The house is largely surrounded by a large expanse of silvery-grey decking, well sheltered from the fierce South African sun, which offers plenty of space for relaxation. Doors on two sides can be folded back for maximum enjoyment of the splendid panorama.

COASTAL TREASURES
Pebbles, shells and other beach finds look compelling arranged on a mantelpiece or in a bowl or jar, especially when displayed against a background of blue-painted wooden boards (*this page & opposite*). The texture and patina of old maritime equipment, such as a cork float or a barnacled anchor, can create beautiful effects.

Display & Collections

Any items that you have a fondness for collecting can form the basis of an eye-catching display. Arranged on my mantelpiece is a herd of mismatched wooden elephants, finely carved, that were found during travels in Africa and Asia; and hanging on my kitchen walls is a varied collection of blue-and-white plates – at least one from each country in Europe that I've visited.

If you live by the sea, you may be fortunate enough to have a world of beautiful objects from nature on your doorstep. Indeed, beachcombing is one of the many pleasures of coastal life, and it is particularly satisfying to adorn your home with shoreline finds – but make sure that you don't remove anything from the beach illegally or damage the coastal ecology.

When choosing which treasures to put on display, consider texture and tactility as much as visual appeal. Wave-smoothed pebbles, limpets and thinly grooved scallop shells arranged on a shelf or windowsill will tempt you to pick them up and stroke them.

By contrast, dried sea sponges and coarse hemp ropes with chunky knots are pleasingly rough to the touch.

Pieces of bleached driftwood, gnarled and contorted into strange shapes, can be smooth or rough, but are often worth treating as works of art, perhaps displayed on a glass shelf or in a vitrine. Tiny pieces of blue and green glass, their edges rubbed smooth by the action of the sea, are amazingly versatile decorative items.

Feathers, starfish and delicate fronds of dried seaweed are ideal for adding form and texture to an interior display. Arrange a row of starfish along a bathroom or kitchen shelf for an instant nautical feel. Shells come in an enormous variety of colours, shapes and sizes, and can be used in myriad ways as containers or to create a decorative effect – glued to mirror frames, strung together to make mobiles, piled into large glass jars or displayed on trays or tabletops with dramatic pink corals.

If you are a genuine sailor – or simply dream about being one – there is no more satisfying way to create the illusion of a life afloat than by displaying nautical paraphernalia in your home. You can transform any space into a veritable ship's cabin by framing old maritime maps and charts behind glass and hanging them on walls, or even covering an entire room with a nautically themed wallpaper.

Old ships' documents are also historically revealing. Victorian-era maps of the River Thames in London, for example, show a bustling waterway crammed with warehouses and docks trading in every imaginable commodity. Alternatively, ocean charts can transport you to an alien underwater world where extraordinary sea creatures thrive.

Paintings and photographs of large expanses of blue ocean are, of course, entirely appropriate in a coastal setting and when cleverly situated they can givethe impression of looking out through an extra 'window' to the sea beyond.

ECOLOGICAL APPROACH
The natural forms of coral offer plenty of inspiration for display in coastal homes and combine harmoniously with other nautically themed objects (*this page & opposite*). The sea often throws up chunks of coral, but it is preferable today to choose faux resin versions for a more eco-friendly approach.

RESCUED FROM EXTINCTION

When Kate Barton discovered The Dodo in 2002, its interior was entirely covered in mud-coloured gloss paint. This was ugly but not surprising, in that the quirkily named house had had a former life as two railway carriages/ railroad cars. Seduced by the history and character of the place, Kate, a fashion designer, embarked on a thorough makeover. The Dodo was rescued from extinction and its brownish-grey plumage replaced with something lighter, brighter and much more appealing.

Overlooking a beach in Sussex, on England's south coast, The Dodo is a relic of a local railway line that was taken out of service in the 1930s. At the time, an unidentified builder decided to locate a couple of defunct train carriages/cars at right angles to the sea, and parallel to each other, and insert a roof over the top of them. Further along the beach are similar houses made in the same way, though it is often difficult to tell from the outside what their origins were. 'One of them is a traditional wooden structure that could very easily be mistaken for a clapboard cottage in Cape Cod,' says Kate.

The generous width of the house and its abundance of glass offered the opportunity to create beautiful, light-filled modern living areas. The bathrooms and four bedrooms are located

STRIKING FOCAL POINTS
From the curved ceiling with its circular moulding to the rows of narrow windows with rounded corners, many elements of the former railway carriage/car are still in evidence. In the principal bedroom (*opposite*), muslin curtains soften the hard lines of the metal four-poster, while blue-and-white-striped bed linen injects vitality into an otherwise subdued tonal scheme. An allium stem in a slim vase, a white bowl full of gastropod shells and some children's paintings serve as striking focal points in the uncluttered interior (*above, left to right*).

GEOMETRIC PATTERNS

Throughout the house, and particularly in the bedrooms, geometric patterns in blinds/shades, bed linens and other fabrics reflect the horizontal and vertical lines of the wall panels and floorboards – and the colour blue is ubiquitous. In one of the children's rooms (*right*), the fitted bunk beds and painted wooden floor evoke the atmosphere of a ship's cabin. In a white-painted guest room (*below*) the Roman blinds/shades and striped bed linen in various tones of blue provide a harmonious and elegant complement to a pair of iron bedsteads.

in the two former carriages/cars, which are linked by a large, open-plan living space heated by a wood-burning stove. As the restoration work got under way, original details were uncovered, from tongue-and-groove panelling to the ceiling friezes. All the walls and ceilings were painstakingly stripped before being painted white. Floorboards were repaired, sanded and also painted white.

After several years, an extension was erected to accommodate a bigger kitchen, a utility area and a downstairs bathroom, as well as an extra bedroom. At the back of the house, a wooden porch with a large skylight was erected, providing direct access to the beach. Kate is particularly proud of her achievement in transforming part of the decked area into a funky outdoor bathroom; the vintage bathtub was picked up at a reclamation yard and there is a hot shower nearby.

A former garage across the road was converted into an annexe containing a playroom and a guest bedroom. There is a tiny garden between the two buildings, which makes a secure play area for small

The two old railway carriages/ railroad cars containing the bedrooms and bathrooms are linked by a split-level living space, which has a wood-burning stove on the lower level (*left*). The walls, ceiling and floor are all painted white. A white cushion with navy stripes softens the rough edges of an indoor bench painted teal blue (*above*).

children. With five bedrooms in the main house and a twin bedroom in the annexe, The Dodo sleeps up to 12 people and is often rented out to large groups of friends. It is also sometimes used as a writers' retreat.

White, white and more white is the decorative theme throughout the house, both inside and out, giving a decorative unity to a structure that was never intended as a home. Wherever colour is introduced, it is almost always a shade of blue, ranging from the slightly sombre teal on benches, chairs and some of the paintwork to the

invigorating sky-blue on the walls in one of the bedrooms. The same sky-blue is used on all the exterior window frames, anchoring the house firmly in its beachside setting.

Bedspreads, pillowcases, cushion covers, curtains and soft furnishings feature geometric patterns, particularly stripes and squares, incorporating a range of blues from across the colour spectrum.

There is a raised dining area with a seagrass carpet, but the family spend most mealtimes on The Dodo's wide deck, enjoying views of the sea.

OUTDOOR BATHROOM

Blue is as much a feature of The Dodo's otherwise white exterior as it is of the interior, with all the window frames painted the same refreshing tone of sky blue (*above & right*). In the decked area, the windows fight for attention with the enormous outdoor bathtub, which was picked up at a reclamation yard. 'I've had ten small children in that bathtub at once,' says Kate. 'They absolutely love it.'

Walls & Ceilings

Walls and ceilings are like the blank canvases in an artist's studio, offering plenty of opportunity to indulge your imagination and give free rein to your creative talents.

If you are starting from scratch, consider the size and proportions of your room and what it will be used for. Is it a public or private space? Could the lighting quality be improved by introducing plenty of white, or by hanging mirrors to reflect natural light? You may have a venerable old house whose vintage character needs preserving, or a bright modern apartment where there is a temptation to experiment with materials, colour and pattern. Alternatively, you may want to defy conventional expectations by mixing old and new. All these elements will feed into decisions about the decorative scheme.

Most ceilings are painted white or a neutral colour, increasing a room's perceived height – an effect that can be emphasized by installing recessed spotlights. Conversely, painting a ceiling midnight blue or another dark colour will make it appear lower. While this may be fine in a private area such as a bedroom or bathroom, it is likely to be oppressive in a living room or kitchen, where a feeling of space and airiness is a priority.

However, painting one wall, or part of a wall, a vivid shade of blue is a spectacular way to add personality to an otherwise bland room. Colour

MODERN TWIST
Period rooms are given a modern twist by bold colour treatments, as in the bedroom of an 18th-century Normandy chateau, where an entire wall of beaded cabinet doors and architraves has been painted floor to ceiling in the same elegant grey-blue (*opposite*). Midnight-blue walls make a wonderful backdrop for an array of fascinating finds picked up at second-hand sales and antiques arcades in southern England (*this page*).

can also be used to make a room seem larger or smaller. Since blue is a receding colour, blue surfaces appear to be further away than they actually are – so, for example, walls painted in an airy sky blue make a room look bigger. While blues can be the coolest hues in the spectrum, they also have a warm and sunny feel, and a pale blue is not necessarily an icy one.

Blue can be a surprisingly dramatic colour when used on its own as a background, but care is needed to gauge the correct depth or saturation of blue required; a shade that's too bright, for instance, could be excessively dominant. Bear in mind that blue-painted walls have the effect of subordinating objects in a room, or making them recede into the background, but they work well with light-coloured wooden furniture or white-dominated displays.

MURAL SCENERY

Walls influence atmosphere – from the funky feel of a hallway with a textural *trompe l'oeil* effect to the cosy intimacy of an all-blue snug (*opposite above*). A subtler result is achieved by delineating the insets of white-painted panels with a thin blue line (*opposite below*). The coolness of a white room with turquoise woodwork/ trim the drama of Popham Design's Hex Target and Scarab tiles and a Cole & Son vintage wallpaper (*this page*).

Flooring

Hard flooring encompasses a wonderfully wide choice of materials, including wood, cork, rubber, slate, stone, marble, concrete, resin, vinyl and tiles of many kinds.

All these materials are available in blue or white versions, or ones that contain elements of blue or white, such as blue-streaked marble or blue-flecked terrazzo tiles. Non-slip cork and rubber are particularly suitable for bathrooms, while vinyl, poured resin and polished concrete are popular in kitchens on account of their smooth good looks and ease of maintenance.

If you want to revive some old weathered floorboards, give them a makeover by sanding and applying limewash to create a translucent milky appearance, or embellish them with a regular white or blue-tinted floor paint. Even some wood-laminate floors are now stained in various shades of blue, from aquamarine to indigo.

In the 19th and early 20th century, there was a fashion for hand-painting tiles with vibrant colours, intricate patterns and motifs to create hardwearing but decorative floors. Original vintage and reproduction tiles are in demand again, with new designs, from tiny mosaics to large slabs, in constant development – and often imitated by linoleum manufacturers.

Plain and patterned rugs add warmth and softness to hard flooring, but don't forget to include a non-slip underlay. Some rugs are big enough to cover an entire floor in place of a carpet, with the advantage that they can be lifted in summer for a cooler feel underfoot.

WOW FACTORS

An innovative idea is to paint bare wooden staircase treads with a central 'stair carpet' of duck-egg blue (*opposite above*). Chevrons and other geometric patterns are useful for delineating different areas (*opposite below & above right*). In a dazzling example of the Popham Design style, a graphic pattern-on-pattern tile scheme enlivens the entrance hall of a Moroccan home (*right*). Geometric floor tiles are great for bathrooms (*above*), while white-painted boards are a classic choice for any room in the house (*far right*).

Rustic

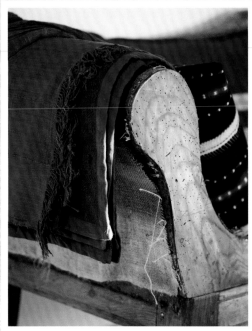

The ideal of country living evokes serene, light-filled spaces, rustic materials and proximity to nature – qualities reflected clearly in homes with an easy transition between indoors and out. Those showcased here include a wooden cottage in Denmark, a historic 'Coffey' house on Fire Island, New York State and a family home in the English Cotswolds. Kitchens and dining rooms are put in the spotlight, along with blue-and-white ceramics and garden retreats.

FARMHOUSE SIMPLICITY

Chalky-white or distressed interior walls and exposed floorboards, some painted white or one of several shades of blue, enhance the rustic character of Mark and Sally Bailey's 18th-century farmhouse near Ross-on-Wye in Herefordshire, on the border between England and Wales. The residence stands next to a cluster of buildings housing the couple's long-established homewares business, Baileys Home Store.

Whitecross Farm is built of local sandstone, with lath and plaster internal walls. As in many old houses, decades of slight movement have caused cracks to appear in walls and ceilings, which display their age in peeling paint and scuffed plasterwork. These imperfect surfaces offer an interesting foundation to any interior design scheme, especially one that foregrounds the combination of blue and white.

Baileys Home Store, the business run by Mark and Sally for more than 35 years, occupies a group of neighbouring barns. Originally in very poor condition, all the buildings, including the farmhouse, have been deliberately restored with minimal impact on their historical integrity and maximum environmental consideration. Keeping the finishes simple throughout, the Baileys used a mixture of materials that included rough lime plaster, raw concrete and uncoated steel.

Mark and Sally describe their business as a general store, stocking an ever-changing

In spite of its depth of colour, indigo can be used to make a subtle statement that isn't overpowering. This corner sofa, backed by mellow, heavily stained ware boards, is covered in a thick blue Belgian linen, complemented by an indigo-dyed rag rug.

collection of homewares, household hardware, stationery, cookware, food, clothing, lighting, antiques and textiles. Before they opened the shop, Mark and Sally had their own architectural antiques business and worked with specialists such as brass and metal founders across the Midlands. These experiences gave them a strong appreciation for craftsmanship, which today is an essential part of the Baileys Home Store ethos. In adopting this philosophy, the Baileys are reflecting their adherence to the tradition established in Victorian times by John Ruskin, William Morris and the Arts and Crafts movement in reaction to the supposed evils of factory production.

Another important influence on the Baileys – which is evident both in their home-decorating adventures and in their store – is the Japanese concept of *wabi-sabi*, which centres on revering humble objects and finding beauty in the imperfect. Much more than just a decorating style, *wabi-sabi* represents a whole world view, examples of which are alive and well in many Japanese homes: the frayed, the weathered and the worn are embraced, and ordinary practical objects are given elevated status by artful display. With care and attention, almost anything can be repaired and reused – far from being disposable, these items tell a story and should be treasured in our homes.

The Baileys' philosophy reveres objects on the basis that they are plain, simple and useful. As well as working with wood-turners, potters, glass-blowers

ARTFUL MIXING
Jute sacking has been stretched over the seat of a chunky wooden bench (*opposite*), which is given a softer look by the addition of indigo-dyed cushions/pillows from Ghana. The traditional resist-dyeing techniques used to make the fabric produce some beautifully uneven results. A cast-concrete shelf (*above*) provides a neutral backdrop for a still life of handmade objects, dominated by blue tones. Bubble glass from Kabul sits alongside celadon and French stoneware and a Japanese raku bowl.

FINISHING TOUCHES
Predominantly white rooms call
for a combination of different
pale tones and textures to make
a more interesting whole. In
this example (*left*), *Thistledown
Coat*, an ethereal painting by
Adrian Bannon, introduces
a ghostly presence above a
stripped-down chesterfield. Two
types of mattress ticking and an
ombré dip-dyed fabric have been
used to cover the cushions/pillows.
Rolls of two-tone thread on top
of a stack of indigo textiles create
a decorative effect; a well-worn
French denim jacket hung against
a paint-stripped door enhances
the wood's textural appeal;
indigo-dyed shepherds' parasols,
closed or open, can work well
as sculptural items; Fog Linen
Work's kitchen cloths, made
in Lithuania, look good when
displayed alone, but their many
different designs are meant to
be mixed and matched (*opposite
clockwise from top left*).

and brush-makers, Mark and Sally also have their our own workshops at the farm, and they
collaborate with small, family-run factories and makers throughout Britain and Europe. Their
wares are unlike anything you would find on the high street. Over the years, the Baileys have
forged their own path and brought together an eclectic array of pieces that they have either
designed themselves or commissioned from small-scale producers. Also in the mix are plenty
of characterful antiques, which sit happily among the handmade items.

Wooden pieces are ubiquitous at Whitecross Farm. In the hallway, blackened ware boards
and old shop signs line the walls, while lamps made from bobbins and plumbers' beads hang
down over the shelf. On the shelf, side by side, stand juggling clubs, pork-pie moulds, turned
bowls and hat blocks. A rustic wooden bench is given a softer look with an arrangement of
cushions/pillows in vegetable-dyed indigo from Ghana. The Baileys are attracted to anything

with a sculptural shape, a curious history or the patina of age, and they like to juxtapose a found wooden object with a decorative one, or place a weather-bleached piece of oak alongside a russet-toned hardwood.

Textiles also feature prominently in the Baileys' home, especially natural materials such as cottons and linens dyed in indigo and other organic shades taken from nature. A strong influence on their choice of fabrics is the Japanese designer Yumiko Sekine, founder of Fog Linen Work, whose creations were inspired by travel to Lithuania, where flax for making linen is grown. One of the many Fog Linen items treasured by the Baileys is a patchwork curtain made from sewn-together kitchen cloths in various renditions of blue and white.

INFORMAL DISPLAYS

A simple metal-framed bedhead (*opposite*) acts as an informal gallery for whatever textiles the Baileys decide to display, such as a collection of Ghanaian tie-dyed indigo throws, hung at different lengths for a deliberately asymmetrical effect. In an intriguing example of *wabi-sabi* (*left*), kitchen towels from Yumiko Sekine's Fog Linen Work have been stitched together to make a patchwork screen. Chalky-white walls diffuse the natural light beautifully (*above left*), with a grey-blue metal lamp and curly iron French bedframe complementing the muted theme. An all-white scheme needs a few dark focal points, such as this indigo batik dressing gown hung on the back of the door (*above*).

Pigments & Dyes

Blue pigments and dyes have been prized by artists and in domestic settings for many hundreds of years.

Pigments were originally made from minerals such as lapis lazuli, cobalt and azurite, and dyes were made from plants – usually woad, which was cultivated throughout Europe, and *Indigofera tinctoria*, or true indigo, originating in Asia and Africa. Today most blue pigments and dyes are manufactured synthetically.

Ultramarine, sometimes called 'true blue', is a pigment made from the gemstone lapis lazuli, once found only in a single mountain range in Afghanistan, making it fabulously expensive. In the 13th century, ultramarine was 'discovered' by Venetian traders and soon became the most sought-after colour in medieval Europe, especially by Renaissance artists.

INTENSE BACKDROP
Panels of deep-dyed indigo
fabric form an intense backdrop
in interiors that reflect *wabi-sabi*
influences from Japanese Zen
Buddhism (*this page & opposite*)
– as in this minimalist 'Japandi'
hallway in Denmark. Adherents
of *wabi-sabi* find beauty in things
that are imperfect, impermanent
and incomplete.

The ancient Romans used the blue of the indigo plant, found in India, to dye furnishing fabrics. Indeed, natural indigo is one of the earliest dyes ever used; India, Japan and West Africa all have a tradition of incorporating it into clothing and other textiles, with the West following the same path after trading routes with those regions had become established.

Indigo was a much-desired commodity throughout the 17th and 18th centuries, driving trade wars between European nations and the Americas. It was used to colour fabrics, clothing, yarns and luxurious tapestries. In contrast to the rarity and expense of ultramarine, indigo came from a plant that was grown in abundance and produced relatively cheaply across the world.

Synthetic indigo is now used to dye denim blue jeans. Recent research has resulted in a method of replicating the chemical reaction that makes indigo in plants, to produce environmentally friendly 'bio indigo'.

INKY-BLUE INTENSITY
These disparate images are united by the rich
saturated blue of the indigo dye – so strong that
it can turn its surroundings to an inky-blue haze.
The jacket, stairs and patchwork curtain seem
almost to vibrate with colour (*opposite*), as do
the tie-dyed African scarves draped over a wall
at a Japanese denim store (*this page*).

TRADITIONAL TEATIME

In an old barn used as a garden shed (*opposite*), the pristine white linen laid with delicate blue-and-white china makes a pleasing contrast to the silvery-grey wooden walls. Lisette's beautiful and practical items include a jug/pitcher from the Portmeirion Botanic Blue collection (*left*) and vintage wall tiles incorporating a Victorian lily motif (*above*).

A DREAM OF OLD ENGLAND

Lisette Pleasance was born and grew up in India – but, entranced by her mother's tales of gardening in her native England, had always dreamed of owning a property in the English countryside. After moving to London, Lisette worked as a landscape gardener, later becoming creative director at Petersham Nurseries in Surrey, and finally realized her dream 15 years ago, when she bought a 16th-century farmhouse near Rye, in East Sussex, in the south-east of England.

Thrilled to have a home with centuries of history, Lisette decided to get rid of recent additions to the interior in order to reveal its original features. Noting the symmetry in the oldest part of the building, she realized that the living room must have had a traditional fireplace identical to the one in the dining room, and when a large area of plasterboard/drywall was taken down she was proved right. Also in this room, wallpaper was removed and carpet pulled up to reveal original floorboards. The classically styled armchairs and footstool have been upholstered in crisp white linen with blue-and-white cushions/pillows. The distressed, white-painted mantelpiece displays a collection of new and old blue pieces.

In a Victorian extension to the main building is the kitchen, where stainless-steel cabinets have

RESCUED AND RECYCLED

The traditional armchairs and footstool in the living room are upholstered in crisp white linen with blue-and-white cushion/ pillow covers (*opposite*), and the unrestored cream mantelpiece is used to display a collection of new and old blue pieces. Willow pattern is found in various shades of blue, but the most common is this deep cobalt blue that was used for the earliest pieces (*far left*). A handwoven linen sheet, paired with handwoven napkins, makes the perfect white tablecloth (*below & left*).

been installed to make an interesting contrast to the traditional Aga range cooker and butcher's block work surface. The utility/laundry room beyond, which includes an antique ironing board and old airing rack, is used to wash and dry the vintage linens that adorn all the beds.

The master bedroom and one of the two guest bedrooms were opened up to the rafters, which have been left exposed. A striking feature of the master bedroom is the elaborate blue-and-white reproduction wallpaper adorning one wall, which incorporates flowers, birds and lush foliage. This Farrow & Ball damask-look design, called St Antoine after the town in France where it was first produced in 1793, makes a powerful statement when paired with the simple wooden beams and bed frame.

Almost all the items brought into the house have been picked up in junk shops, at auction houses or in salvage yards, and adapted to perform new roles. Beautiful old window frames have been fitted with mirrors, for example, and, in one particularly successful haul, a £1 bag of oddments of Venetian glass turned out to be the makings of a magnificent chandelier.

Lisette's partner, Mick Shaw, is a builder who shares her love of salvaged objects. He has incorporated reclaimed materials into the house, using vintage doors to conceal fitted storage shelves, and repurposing timber from a dilapidated shed to box in the pipework in the master bathroom. Some of the furniture is also made by Mick, including a dining table crafted from 16th-century boards rescued from a building project.

Achieving a classic rustic style means using elements that have stood the test of time – and Lisette has a talent for using vintage fabrics in her interiors to convey an unpretentious, lived-in look. Hand-loomed linen tablecloths, embroidered French sheets and monogrammed napkins – all in blue and white – make for an elegance that is truly ageless. Whether scouring antiques shops or exploring internet sites, she is always on the lookout for bone-handled knives, silver-plated cutlery/ flatware and other table treasures to add to her collection.

SOPHISTICATION AND DRAMA
Based on an 18th-century damask-look design, originally produced at St Antoine in France, a modern reproduction wallpaper introduces an aura of sophistication into an otherwise rustic bedroom (*above*). Equally eye-catching is the wallpaper on the ceiling of the upstairs landing (*left*), reproduced from a pattern found at Uppark, an 18th-century English country house in West Sussex whose interior was designed by Sir Matthew Fetherstonhaugh. The startling contrast between the soft blue and white of the papered ceiling and the black of the cast-iron lantern adds drama to an area that is often given little attention when decorating a house. In the bathroom (*opposite*), the rusting ball-and-claw feet of the Victorian bathtub testify to its age. The cool aquamarine tones of the room, taken up in the coordinating towels and textured bathmat, are offset by the warmth of the natural wooden floorboards, beams and sturdy chair.

CHIC PRACTICALITY
A run of kitchen cabinets
in duck-egg blue, set against
a row of darker grey-blue
drawers, combines elegance
with practicality (*this page*).
In many country kitchens,
checks are indispensable
– in the form of chair
covers, kitchen towels,
tablecloths or gingham
half-curtains hung to hide
pots and pans (*opposite*).

Kitchens & Dining

There is a host of ways, big and small, to combine blue and white in your kitchen. These could include painting an entire wall a deep Matisse blue, while leaving the ceiling and skirting boards/baseboards white; dressing the dining table with a cheerful blue-and-white checked tablecloth; or simply placing a row of striped storage jars on a shelf.

Although blue is a receding colour, darker shades can be overpowering when used to cover large areas, so proceed with care. More restrained alternatives to the whole-wall approach might include, for example, choosing a blue-fronted range cooker and refrigerator to set against a white background, or installing a blue-veined marble countertop and a run of kitchen cabinets in duck-egg blue.

No space is more likely than a country kitchen to provide the right setting for painted and distressed wooden furniture, particularly an antique dresser/hutch, which can be used to display collections of glass bottles, blue-and-white plates and other china items. Wooden chairs, tables and window frames can also be painted pale blue and, if exposed to natural light, allowed to fade to silvery grey as they mature.

Apart from white and terracotta, blue is the most common colour to be seen in Delft tiles, Moroccan tiles and Mexican Talavera tiles – all of which bring elements of beauty and vitality to expanses of wall, and are especially useful behind hobs/stovetops and sinks, where splashback protection is needed. Floors, too, can be given their share of blue, whether in the form of paint, poured concrete, tiles or vinyl flooring.

DEGREES OF SUBTLETY
Blue can work in subtle and not-so-subtle ways in dining spaces and kitchens – from the palest of pale sky blues in textured walls or a cooker casing (*opposite*) to the zingy turquoise of walls and tiles in a corner used for washing dishes (*above left*). Patterned blue-and-white plates, soup tureens and storage jars are favourite items for display (*above & left*), and checks are ubiquitous (*far left*).

Since the kitchen is a room that's naturally full of hard surfaces, straight lines and plain, often neutral colours, introducing colourful fabrics creates a welcome contrast of warmth and softness, pattern and texture, and injects interesting touches that brighten and add comfort to the space. Single-coloured fabrics that complement an understated modern kitchen or dining area look just as effective as country-style ginghams or florals in a more rustic space.

Every dining chair, stool and bench should be a pleasure to sit on, so consider adding firm cushions/pillows to wooden or moulded-plastic seats. Box-shaped examples, secured to a chair with ties, provide excellent padding. Blue-and-white seat covers and cushions/pillows can be used to unify a group of otherwise disparate chairs and, if the fabric design is interesting,

they can even become a focal point of the decorative scheme. Loosely fitting seat covers made from white or off-white cotton or linen will disguise ugly chairs and unify mismatching sets.

Gathered gingham is ideal in a country kitchen, both for window curtains and in fabric panels used to screen low cupboards or utilitarian items on shelves or under a sink. And gingham has other purposes too. Scraps of vintage floral and gingham fabric can be repurposed to make attractive napkins, for example.

Fabric accessories proliferate in many kitchens, with kitchen towels top of the list; choose a few matching ones with the classic blue-on-white stripe or a more modern pattern. Other accessories in blue and white could include tray cloths, linings for storage boxes, hand towels, oven gloves/mitts, aprons and tea cosies.

DANISH SUMMER COTTAGE

Like many other city-living Danes, Else and Keld Jorgensen frequently retreat in summer to the countryside – in their case, to a simple wooden cottage in Tisvildelej, a village on the north coast of Zealand, not far from the shores of the Kattegat Sea. Its exterior is painted falu red, a colour widely seen on rural buildings in Scandinavia.

DINING IN STYLE

Alfresco meals are enjoyed on a large wooden deck (*left*), where contrasting shades of blue are evident in the tablecloth, cushion/pillow covers, ceramics and floor mat. The terrace overlooks the garden and an annexe for guests (*above*), which, like the house, is painted falu red. In the open-plan kitchen (*opposite*), striped slipcovers have been used to protect the chair seats in the dining area.

Built on former farmland, the Jorgensen home consists of 55 square metres/600 square feet of open-plan living space, including kitchen, dining area and sitting room, and an L-shaped wraparound deck – providing the perfect spot for enjoying long alfresco lunches.

The interior decorative scheme is deliberately relaxed and understated. Light-coloured wooden floors and an A-frame ceiling enhance the clean, airy lines of the main living room, from where double glass doors lead onto the terrace. There is a bedroom at each end of this area and a third bedroom in the garden annex.

In keeping with classic Scandinavian style, all the walls and ceilings have been painted white to reflect the natural light. A collection of blue-and-white cushions/pillows with varying patterns, including ikat, stonewash and stripes, makes the

THE APPEAL OF AZURE

Azure tiles with pristine white grouting perfectly match the 1960s cabinets in the kitchen (*opposite*), setting the colour theme for the whole house; in front of the chopping/cutting board is a set of blue-and-white ceramics from Normann Copenhagen. Above the sink, a pair of candy-stripe kitchen towels has been transformed into curtains, secured by wooden pegs/clothespins (*below*). Flashes of blue can also been seen in the china and glassware on the floor-to-ceiling shelving (*above right*) and in other displays (*above left*).

sofas more inviting. An industrial-style pendant from IKEA and a classic floor lamp found at a flea market light up the space at night.

When remodelling the kitchen, the Jorgensens decided to keep the retro cabinet doors installed in the 1960s because their striking azure blue works beautifully with the crisp white walls. Matching blue tiles with white grout were added, setting the colour theme for the whole interior, and ceramics and glass on display often include dashes of blue.

Blue accents are evident in other rooms – in cushions/pillows, rugs, bed linen and more. Throughout the house, Scandinavian antiques and local vintage finds are juxtaposed with high-street purchases and Danish designer pieces to make a fascinating blend of old and new.

A UNIFYING THEME

Pebbles from a nearby beach (*above left*) make a beautiful display on top of the midnight-blue wood-burning stove in the living room (*opposite*). The tiles under the stove are a similar shade of blue. A handmade bamboo basket from Oi Soi Oi, used to store striped outdoor seat pads, and a blue-rimmed copper tray add interest to a sitting area (*left, right & above*). The variety of covers on the sofa cushions/pillows – some striped, some stonewashed, some in an ikat fabric – are unified by a blue-and-white theme, and teamed with a blue-striped rug.

Ceramics

Patterned blue-and-white ceramics are both aesthetically pleasing and highly practical, offering a huge range of opportunities for adding decorative interest to any home.

They have a long history too, first becoming popular in the West in the 18th century, with the export from China of Nanking porcelain featuring a brilliant deep-blue colour made from a purified salt of cobalt. Powder blue was originally obtained by blowing powdered cobalt onto the surface of the porcelain. The ubiquitous 'ginger jar', produced in China from ancient times to store provisions such as oil, salt and spices, is a classic design that is still being made today.

Willow-pattern china was conceived and made by Thomas Minton in 1780 in response to the contemporary fashion in England for all things Chinese. The original design has a waterside scene in a garden, a pavilion, figures on a bridge and a central pair of birds.

Willow pattern is found in many different iterations and many different tones of blue, and even in browns and blacks, but the most common is the striking deep cobalt blue that was used for the earliest pieces.

CLASSIC STYLES
Wedgwood and willow-pattern jugs/pitchers, bowls and vases combine well with oriental-style and contemporary blue-and-white ceramics. These classic styles are perfectly at home in traditional and modern settings alike (*this page & opposite*).

PATTERN MIX
A cornucopia of mismatched antique tableware in a weathered oak kitchen dresser/hutch makes an appealing display when linked by a blue-and-white theme (*this page*). In this rustic kitchen the theme is reflected in a strip of Delft-style tiles behind the cooker. Some items of buff-coloured caneware introduce light relief. Blue-and-white ceramics often have traditional patterns (*opposite above left & right*) but a selection of abstract vases offers a more modern take on mixing (*opposite below*).

Meanwhile, after years of experimentation, Josiah Wedgwood produced in 1775 the first examples of jasperware, a unique form of stoneware coloured with metal oxides and characterized by an unglazed 'biscuit' finish and white bas-relief decorations. It was made in several different colours, of which the most common and most distinctive is a pale blue that has become known as Wedgwood blue.

Josiah Spode, another English pioneer in the field, perfected in 1784 a technique for transfer printing onto earthenware using engraved copper plates. His Blue Italian ware, in production ever since, has become one of the most collectible ranges in history.

There are as many designs of blue-and-white plates as there are potteries, and china made by Minton, Spode, Wedgwood and others, as well as by a host of lesser-known makers, has always been very sought after.

Other countries have equally strong traditions of ceramic production. For example, a combination of blue and white has been used in the decoration of Moroccan ceramics since the 13th century, and in the mid 19th century a dramatic cobalt blue was introduced that is still popular today.

The city of Fez is particularly well known for its blue-and-white pottery known as bleu de Fez, or Moroccan blue. The colour became predominant on account of the large deposits of cobalt that were to be found in the rocks and stones swept down by the rivers, which were ground down to provide the blue powder used in glazes.

A FRESH LOOK AT COUNTRY STYLE

Nick and Vanessa Arbuthnott have transformed three interconnected farm buildings in the English Cotswolds into a beautiful family home that combines classic country style with easy practicality. Built from mellow Cotswold stone, the original one-storey structure looks from the exterior very much as it always has done – but inside everything has changed.

The group of disused buildings had previously accommodated a cowshed and two piggeries. When the Arbuthnotts moved in, there was no mains electricity, so for more than a year they depended on a noisy generator. They also had to survive for a while with no internal doors, but gradually the house took shape. Nick is an architect who specializes in renovating old rural buildings with minimal external intervention. He designed a home that kept as much as possible of the original structure, reusing old materials where feasible and adding new elements with sensitivity. He created a hallway, a study, the kitchen and a studio for Vanessa, who designs hand-printed fabrics. Bedrooms and bathrooms, all with sloping ceilings, were inserted into the roof space, with roof lights set into the old tiles.

COOL AND ELEGANT

The Arbuthnotts' doors and windows are painted with an eggshell finish in a cool, elegant azure blue – popular as a 'heritage' colour (*left & opposite*). Exterior paintwork needs to survive the onslaughts of the weather, so choose a paint that is resistant to peeling and flaking but still allows the wood to breathe. Violet and white violas in terracotta pots provide a vibrant contrast to the blue doors (*above*).

Despite its spaciousness and elegance, the house exudes friendly informality. The two staircases, for example, have been used as goalposts in many a game of football/soccer, while the kitchen is the 'everything room', where parents and children spend most of their time. When Vanessa and Nick were working on the house, their four children were all under six years old and demanded a huge amount of attention. 'It felt as if we were always racing against time,' says Vanessa. 'We quickly slapped on the paint in room after room, and made use of furniture from our previous home, buying very little new stuff and simply mending things where necessary.'

Downstairs, French double doors have been let into the deep stone walls all around, opening out into the inner

courtyard and garden, and allowing access to the outside from all areas of the house. These traditional items were acquired at a home store in Calais and shipped back to England. The Arbuthnotts decided to paint all the external paintwork azure blue because of its evocation of Mediterranean summer skies; the overall effect is reminiscent of a romantic old farmhouse in the depths of Provence.

In the entrance hall, stripped floorboards, skirting boards/baseboards and stairs are all painted an invigorating aquamarine, creating a swathe of colour that sweeps along the woodwork/trim and up the curving staircase, subtly offset by creamy-white walls.

The blue-and-white combination reaches its climax in the living room, where icy-blue walls are sharpened by chalky-white floorboards and slightly creamier wooden features, including a moulded mantelpiece and a narrow coffee table. The blue of the walls is one of a range of heritage paint colours inspired by the decoration of grand country houses of the past.

It is the use of fabrics, however, that gives the living room its quintessentially country look. Stripes are mixed with naturally inspired motifs, such as cow parsley, fern leaves and swallows, bringing the themes and colours of the countryside inside, to be enjoyed as much in winter as in summer. Blues and whites are softened by their juxtaposition with the earthier hues of the Cotswold stone fireplace and the striped sofa fabric.

Indeed, whatever style of house you live in, the adoption of a unifying blue-and-white theme makes it possible to bring together a wide range of patterns, plains and geometrics.

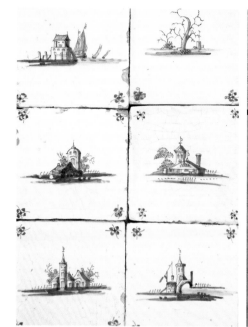

MATCHING AND MIXING

Stripped floorboards, woodwork and stairs in the entrance hall (*opposite above*) are all painted in the same shade of aquamarine – a colour picked out in the paintings hanging on the cream walls. The stairs provide a platform for the display of blue-and-white enamel jugs/pitchers (*opposite below*), used for carrying hot water in the days before modern plumbing.

Items that the Arbuthnotts like to collect include blue-and-white Delftware decorated with hand-painted motifs depicting Dutch life (*top left*) and later imitations such as these tiles reclaimed from a Victorian washstand (*top right*). Willow-pattern china (*above right*) remains hugely popular in country homes, as do traditional striped mugs and plates (*above left*).

EASY HARMONY
Combining patterns is easy with a blue-and-white theme. In the airy living room (*left*), various designs inspired by nature work together because their shared dominant colour is a pale sky blue. Blues and whites harmonize with the raw earthy shades of the Cotswold stone fireplace, and this colour mix is reflected in the stone and blue of the sofa fabric. An oriental-style teapot on the mantelpiece looks at home beside a vintage Delft tile (*above*).

Garden Retreats

The joy of a garden is a compelling reason for living in the countryside, and most people with a garden like to reserve a special outdoor space, however large or small, for sitting, dining, relaxing and making the most of the verdant surroundings.

Your outdoor space may be a porch attached to the house, a brick patio or paved terrace, a wooden deck or simply somewhere in the garden under a tree or near the sound of running water – or it could consist of a more permanent structure such as a pergola, gazebo or open-sided summerhouse, even somewhere quite distant from the house itself.

An outdoor corner can be as inviting as one inside, and it deserves to be furnished and decorated with as much care. There is a surprisingly wide variety of furniture in various shades of blue that is custom-made for patios and verandas, from benches, tables, stools and sunbeds to chairs of all types – wooden, metal, wicker,

STRUCTURAL FORMS

Blue-painted structures, such as doors and window frames, will give form and definition to your garden retreat, and painted metal bistro chairs and tables create a relaxed air (*this page & opposite*). White varieties of geranium, agapanthus and hydrangea look great in chunky square planters. Blue-and-white china with a fish design and striped plant pots bring a table setting alive, while small blue flowers such as myosotis and various herbs are good for decoration.

JOYS OF NATURE
Make a splash in your outdoor space with a slatted-back bench and wooden table painted vibrant turquoise (*far left*), or with a supersized blue-and-white-checked tablecloth set for an alfresco lunch (*opposite*). The hard-edged appearance of garden furniture can be softened by adding comfortable seat pads (*below*). Allow nature to invade in the shape of colourful plants in pots (*left*) or a border of fragrant lavender that is bound to prove irresistible to bees.

wrought iron, plastic and more. Or you can make your own by painting or staining old wooden or metal chairs and bistro tables in a shade of your choice.

These pieces can be softened in appearance and made more comfortable by padded seats covered in white linen or an array of striped, checked or patterned cushions/pillows. An old garden table can be refreshed by the addition of a crisp white or checked tablecloth.

Alfresco dining opens up a wide range of possibilities for table settings – in the form of matching or mismatching blue-and-white plates, cups and saucers, bowls and mugs. You might want to include blue-handled cutlery/flatware or blue glass drinking vessels and jugs/pitchers. Small glass or china vases filled with freshly cut spring or summer flowers make delightful finishing touches.

Patios and verandas are ideal locations for hanging baskets, terracotta pots and wooden tubs planted with your favourite shrubs and annuals. Ideally, your outdoor space will also be in close proximity to colourful garden flowers and trees.

If you want to plan your plantings according to a blue-and-white theme, there are an endless number of possible combinations. Blues range from vivid periwinkles, asters, lisianthus and delphiniums to

deep-purple violas and gentians; while whites might include dianthus, campanula, agapanthus and roses. White geraniums look great in a bright-blue pot or a wooden planter painted sky blue. Alternatively, you could train a climbing white rose over an arbour and pair it with a purplish-blue clematis.

CALM AFTER THE STORM

The small town of Saltaire on Fire Island, which runs parallel with the southern shore of Long Island, is famous for its distinctive 'Coffey' houses, designed in the early 20th century by Mike Coffey, an Irish émigré who became the town's master builder. His cedar-shingled, light-filled buildings are admired for their seamless melding of beauty and functionality.

LIGHT-FILLED PORCH

A wooden boardwalk (*above centre*) leads from the beach to the entrance of the house, a covered porch, where guests are greeted by a selection of quirky objects (*above left & right*), including a handbell that must be rung to signal arrival, an aquamarine enamel bucket and, hanging by the door, an assortment of playful signs. Lined on two sides by windows, the porch has blue rattan chairs and built-in window seating with blue-and-white cushions/pillows, which not only makes a cosy place for relaxation but also provides extra sleeping space for guests (*opposite*).

Starting in 1910 and working over a long period, Coffey was responsible for more than 100 Saltaire houses, the community hall, three churches and an extension to the yacht club. Many structures were destroyed in the Great New England Hurricane of 1938, but some survive and remain in use today. One recurrent architectural feature is a triple vertical pattern in the upper part of the windowpane, referred to locally as an 'eyebrow' window.

Among the survivors is a building that is now the home of Alex and Andrew Bates, who have been visiting Fire Island since the early 1990s. They loved the peace and solitude of the island, combined with its proximity to New York City, where both held down demanding jobs. The couple had always been attracted to the rustic character of the Coffey houses, and they eventually acquired one of their own. 'We've kept our Coffey house true to the original design,' says Alex.

They retained the floor plan and the original kitchen and, apart from replacing some old tiles with wood panelling, they initially preserved everything just as it was when they found it, including the Matisse-blue linoleum floor in the kitchen. The decorative style was kept simple so that the house would be easy to maintain. Most of the interiors were painted white, to make the most of the natural light, and the furniture – a mix of found pieces and family heirlooms – was covered in washable white slipcovers. The main living room has a traditional fireplace with a brick surround and chimneypiece, both of which were painted glossy white, in keeping with the rest of the room.

One of the spectacular features of the house is the large enclosed entrance porch that doubles as an additional living space, with several other rooms leading off it. The cedar shingles on the exterior façade are continued into the interior of this room, where they have been stained a rich chocolate brown, in stark contrast to the white-painted

SIMPLICITY ITSELF

The decision to adopt a simple decorative style so that the house would be easy to maintain is particularly evident in the main living room (*above*). Most of the furniture is second-hand, and the sofas and chairs are covered in washable white cotton slipcovers, creating a relaxed mood. Glossy white paint on walls, doors and ceilings makes the most of the natural light that streams in from the verdant garden. Flashes of blue can be detected in the jug/pitcher on the coffee table, in the spines of books and in the striped-ticking cushion/pillow covers. The room's only flamboyant element is visible above the mantelpiece (*opposite*), where a mirror framed with a variety of shiny white shells hangs beside a pair of translucent aquamarine glass containers.

floor, ceiling and window frames. The porch includes built-in window seats that can be used as beds when the house is full of guests.

Restoration work was required in 2012, following the flooding on Fire Island caused by Hurricane Sandy, and Alex and Andrew used the opportunity to carry out some major improvements, but they kept the wooden floors because they like the naturally occurring 'cupping' of the boards.

'The whole project was like building a house from the inside out,' says Alex. 'We moved a couple of walls to straighten out some original awkward angles, and installed all-new electric wiring and heating.' They designed the new spaces to feel modern but also in a way that was respectful of the house's original spirit. Fortunately, the only repair needed to the outside of the house was the replacement of some cedar shingles.

For the people of Saltaire, the worst effect of the hurricane was that gardens that had been planted and carefully tended over many years were destroyed by the floods, along with a multitude of trees. For the past decade, local inhabitants have been working hard to restore these gardens to their former glory.

KITCHEN CONTRASTS
The kitchen is connected to the living room by a narrow arched opening that frames the Matisse-blue linoleum floor and the blue-painted farmhouse table and chairs (*opposite*). When the restoration work was under way, Alex decided to retain the flooring to provide a vibrant contrast with the otherwise all-white interior (*above*). A plate rack stacked with pretty, blue-flecked oyster platters and a row of upturned greenish-blue glasses creates an arresting visual display behind the table (*above left*).

EARTHY SCHEME
The cedar shingles used to clad the outside of the house were continued into the porch, where they have been stained earthy brown, in contrast to the white-painted floor, ceiling and woodwork/trim (*opposite*). Striped and patterned seat covers, throws and pillows in the bedroom leading off the porch enliven the otherwise subdued palette (*this page*).

Decorating with Flowers

Houseplants and cut flowers can be used throughout the year to add vivid splashes of blue to an otherwise neutral interior scheme and brighten up even the darkest days.

Choose pots and vases that are either colourful enough to match the blooms they hold or understated enough to fade into the background, allowing the flowers to take centre stage.

Weathered or chipped containers can be given a new lease of life when planted with hyacinth bulbs for winter flowering. Plant in the early autumn in bulb potting mix and add a little water. Keep in a cool, dark place until the shoots are 5 centimetres/2 inches high, then bring into a warm room and keep moist until they bloom.

Blue muscari, or grape hyacinths, are one of the earliest garden plants to flower in spring, soon followed by anemones and flag irises. Summer brings a host of plants that produce good flowers for cutting, including sea holly, cornflower and campanula. Some houseplants – such as hydrangeas, which dry out quickly when cut – are best left to grow in containers.

SPRINGING TO LIFE
There is no better way to celebrate the season of new life than by arranging a bunch of spring flowers such as purplish-blue anemones (*far right*) in a vase or jug/pitcher. As the year progresses, the choice of blue-and-white flowers becomes wider (*right, below & below right*), but some plants, such as hydrangeas, thrive better in containers (*opposite*). Hydrangeas produce blue flowers only when grown in soil with high acidity; otherwise the blooms are usually white or pink.

SOURCES

FABRICS & HOMEWARES

Burford Garden Co
www.burford.co.uk
*Cushions, throws and rugs
with a country theme.*

Cabbages & Roses
www.cabbagesandroses.com
*Floral curtains, bed linens
and wallpapers.*

Caravane
www.caravane.co.uk
*French-inspired bed linen,
tableware, lighting and
furniture.*

Cath Kidston
www.cathkidston.com
*Vintage-style fabrics
and home accessories.*

Coco & Wolf
www.cocoandwolf.com
*Liberty fabrics for the bedroom,
dining room and living room.*

Designers Guild
www.designersguild.com
*Bold modern designs for fabrics,
wallpapers, bed linen and rugs.*

Garnet Hill
www.garnethill.com
*Specialist in fabrics for
bedrooms and bathrooms.*

Ian Mankin
www.ianmankin.co.uk
*Striped, checked, floral and
plain designs for curtains
and soft furnishings.*

Inchyra
www.inchyra.com
*Timeless fabrics and accessories
from the Scottish Highlands.*

Jan Constantine
www.janconstantine.com
*Hand-embroidered cushion/
pillow covers, many with a
celebratory theme.*

Lewis & Wood
www.lewisandwood.co.uk
*Classic and unusual fabrics,
toiles and wallpapers.*

Lexington
www.lexingtoncompany.com
*Bed linen, bath towels and
kitchen accessories.*

Liberty London
www.libertylondon.com
*Luxury fabrics, designer
furniture and stylish homewares.*

Rachel Ashwell Shabby Chic
www.shabbychic.com
*Furniture and homewares
that celebrate romance
and nostalgia.*

Ralph Lauren Home
www.ralphlaurenhome.com
*Fabrics, wall coverings and floor
coverings combining vintage
elegance with modern styling.*

Soak & Sleep
www.soakandsleep.com
*Bedspreads, throws and
cushion covers.*

The Cloth Shop
www.theclothshop.net
*A large selection of fabrics,
linens and quilts.*

The Linen Works
www.thelinenworks.com
*Striped fabrics and items
for bedroom, kitchen
and bathroom.*

The Stripes Company
www.thestripescompany.com
*Striped-fabric specialists
– deckchairs, curtains, blinds/
shades, cushions and throws.*

Vanessa Arbuthnott
www.vanessaarbuthnott.co.uk
*Fabrics and wallpapers inspired
by the natural world.*

West Elm
www.westelm.co.uk
Sofas, cushions and rugs.

FURNITURE, LIGHTING, FLOORING & ACCESSORIES

ABC Carpet & Home
www.abchome.com
*Everything for the home
in this New York emporium,
vintage and modern.*

Baileys Home Store
www.baileyshome.com
*An ever-changing collection
of homewares, lighting,
antiques and textiles, based
on a philosophy of recycling.*

Barn Light Electric Company
www.barnlight.com
*Vintage-inspired enamel
lighting – pendants, chandeliers
and table lamps.*

Blue Dot Pottery
polishpotteryshop.co.uk
Fine handmade Polish pottery.

Buy the Sea
www.buythesea.co.uk
*Driftwood furniture and
mirrors.*

Crate & Barrel
www.crateandbarrel.com
*A huge range of furniture,
lighting and homewares for
indoor and outdoor living.*

Flooring America
www.flooringamerica.com
*Hardwood, vinyl, tiles, carpet
and more.*

FRP Homestore
www.frphomestore.com
*Cushions/pillows, lighting and
tableware curated by the
interior designer Francesca
Rowan Plowden.*

Graham and Green
www.grahamandgreen.co.uk
*Furniture, lighting, mirrors
and rugs.*

House of Hackney
www.houseofhackney.com
*Wallpapers, fabrics, blinds/
shades and rugs.*

John Derian
www.johnderian.com
*Antique blue-and-white
ceramics; new interpretations
of vintage fabric designs.*

Labour and Wait
www.labourandwait.co.uk
*Enamelled kitchen items
and utilitarian glassware.*

Odd Limited
www.oddlimited.com
Garden furniture and fabrics.

RH
www.rh.com
*Formerly known as Restoration
Hardware, this company also
has an exceptional range of
furniture, textiles and lighting.*

Roger Oates Design
www.rogeroates.com
Runners and rugs.

Rothschild & Bickers
www.rothschildbickers.com
Vintage and modern lighting.

Scumble Goosie
www.scumblegoosie.co.uk
*Mango-wood furniture, sold
either painted or unpainted.*

Serena & Lily
www.serenaandlily.com
*California-themed furniture,
bed linen, wallpaper and
home accessories ideal
for beachside living.*

**The Best Adirondack
Chair Company**
www.thebestadirondack
chair.com
*Handcrafted, solid-wood
Adirondack chairs for porches
and outdoor spaces.*

**The Coastal
Lifestyle Company**
www.thecoastallifestyle
company.co.uk
*Furniture and accessories
for home and garden, all
with a coastal flavour.*

**The English Panelling
Company**
www.theenglishpanelling
company.co.uk
*Bespoke panelling to add
character to interiors.*

ANTIQUES

City Foundry
www.cityfoundry.com
*Antique furniture of all
kinds for home and garden
in Brooklyn's Industry City.*

French General Trading
www.frenchgeneral
trading.co.uk
*French rustic furniture
and decorative antiques.*

Hoof Brocante
www.hoofbrocante.com
*French antiques, furniture
and fabrics.*

Pale & Interesting
www.paleandinteresting.com
*Furniture, including a 'coast
collection', fabrics, lighting,
glassware.*

Quirky Interiors
www.quirkyinteriors.co.uk
*Specialist in industrial and
vintage furniture, aged zinc
and other vintage items.*

Susan Deliss
www.susandeliss.com
*Antique suzanis, kilims
and other textiles.*

The Mart Collective
www.themartcollective.com
*Los Angeles antiques market –
a great source for everything
vintage, from furniture to textiles
to decorative accessories.*

PAINTS & WALLPAPERS

Annie Sloan
www.anniesloan.com

Benjamin Moore
www.benjaminmoore.com

Cole & Son
www.cole-and-son.com

Edward Bulmer Natural Paint
www.edwardbulmerpaint.co.uk

Farrow & Ball
www.farrow-ball.com

Lick
www.lick.com

Little Greene
www.littlegreene.com

Morris & Co and Sanderson
www.sandersondesigngroup.com

Paint & Paper Library
www.paintlibrary.co.uk

Papers and Paints
www.papers-paints.co.uk

PICTURE CREDITS

Key: Ph = photographer; a = above; b = below; l = left; c = centre;
r = right.

1 Ph Lisa Cohen/The designer Clare Teed's home in Hampton,
www.sashawaddelldesign.com; 2 Ph Mark Lohman; 3 Ph Catherine
Gratwicke; 4–5 Ph Rachel Whiting/The home of interior journalist
and blogger Jill Macnair in London; 7 al Ph Benjamin Edwards/
'Nautilus' is the home in Cornwall of James and Lisa Bligh
www.uniquehomestays.com; 7 ar Ph Rachel Whiting/Saša Antic –
interior stylist, set and props; 7 bl Ph James Gardiner/Jeska and
Dean Hearne of thefuturekept.com; 7 br Ph Polly Wreford/The
family home of Derek and Elsbeth Rankin; 8 Ph Polly Wreford/
Foster House, the family home of Atalanta Bartlett and Dave
Coote, available to hire through www.beachstudios.co.uk; 9 Ph Debi
Treloar/The family home of designers Ulla Koskinen and Sameli
Rantanen in Finland; 10 Ph Debi Treloar/The home of the film
director Christina Höglund in Österlen, Sweden; 11 Ph Debi Treloar/
Okura; 12–13 Ph Jan Baldwin/The home of Françoise Piccino of La
Cabane de Jeanne; 14 l Ph Mark Scott; 14 c Ph Polly Wreford/
Paul's beach house in Sussex, Design www.davecoote.com; 14 r Ph
Christopher Drake; 15 Ph Debi Treloar/Country house, Suffolk;
16–21 Ph Debi Treloar/The home of the antique textiles dealer
Katharine Pole in London; 22 a Ph Polly Wreford/Ros Fairman's
house in London; 22 b Ph Mark Scott; 23 Ph Debi Treloar/Country
house, Suffolk; 24 al Ph Debi Treloar/The home of the film director
Christina Höglund in Österlen, Sweden; 24 ar Ph Debi Treloar/Fog
Linen Work; 24 bl Ph Amy Neunsinger; 24 br Ph Benjamin
Edwards/The Old Coastguard House – home of Martin and Jane
Will; 25 a Ph Mark Lohman; 25 b Ph Lisa Cohen/Clara Baillie's
house on the Isle of Wight; 26–33 Ph Benjamin Edwards/Elena
Colombo; 34 a Ph Polly Wreford/The Sussex home of Paula
Barnes of www.elizabarnes.com; 34 b Ph Simon Brown; 35 al Ph
Christopher Drake; 35 ar Ph Catherine Gratwicke; 35 bl Ph Mark
Scott; 35 br Ph Keith Scott Morton; 36 a Ph Hans Blomquist;
36 b Ph Debi Treloar/Mark and Sally Bailey's home in
Herefordshire; 37 al Ph Gavin Kingcome/William Yeoward;
37 ar Ph Gavin Kingcome/William Yeoward; 37 b Ph Earl Carter/
Interior design by Janet Kielley Interiors and architecture by
Luke Thornewill Designs; 38–45 Ph Mark Scott; 46 Ph Polly
Wreford/Beauty Point and Coast House available to hire through
www.beachstudios.co.uk; 47 a Ph Benjamin Edwards/The Shack
available as a shoot location www.lordshippark.com; 47 b Ph
Benjamin Edwards/The Old Coastguard House – home of Martin
and Jane Will; 48 al Ph Debi Treloar/Pip Rau; 48 ar Ph Simon
Brown; 48 bl Ph Benjamin Edwards/The Ferryman's and The
Saltbox are situated on the Elmley Nature Reserve and available to
rent www.elmleynaturereserve.co.uk; 48 br Ph Simon Brown;
49 l Ph Benjamin Edwards/The home of conscious entrepreneurs
Gesine and Gerry Haag in Mallorca; 49 r Ph Mark Scott; 50–55
Ph Rachel Whiting/The home of Maria Carr of Dreamy Whites

www.dreamywhitesatelier.com; 56 al Ph Polly Wreford/Lena
Proudlock's house in Gloucestershire; 56 ar Ph Simon Upton/
Jacomini Interior Design, Texas; 56 bl Ph Simon Brown; 56 br Ph
Gavin Kingcome; 57 a Ph Gavin Kingcome; 57 b Ph Polly Wreford/
The family home of Sarah and Mark Benton in Rye; 58 ar Ph Hans
Blomquist; 58 br Ph Emma Mitchell; 59 al Ph Keith Scott Morton;
59 ar Ph Benjamin Edwards/The home of conscious entrepreneurs
Gesine and Gerry Haag in Mallorca; 59 bl Ph Polly Wreford/The
home of the designer Anne Geistdoerfer; 59 br Ph Catherine
Gratwicke/The home of Hanne Borge in Norway; 60–67 Ph Jan
Baldwin/Laurence and Yves Sabouret's house in Brittany;
68 al Ph Amy Neunsinger; 68 ar Ph Christopher Drake; 68 bl Ph
Christopher Drake; 69 al Ph Jan Baldwin/Elizabeth Machin's
Norfolk cottage; 69 ar Ph Debi Treloar/The home of Tim Rundle;
69 b Ph Debi Treloar/Debbie Johnson of Powder Blue – styling,
props, locations www.powder-blue.co.uk; 70–71 Ph Earl Carter/
The home of Cary Tamarkin and Mindy Goldberg on Shelter Island;
72 l Ph Benjamin Edwards; 72 c Ph Paul Massey/The Spreitzer
Residence, Southampton, New York; 72 r Ph Paul Massey; 73 Ph
Paul Massey/The home in Denmark of Charlotte Lynggaard,
designer of Ole Lynggaard; 74–79 Ph Benjamin Edwards/The beach
hideaway in Javea designed by Jessica Bataille www.jessicabataille.
com; 80 al Ph Benjamin Edwards/The home of conscious
entrepreneurs Gesine and Gerry Haag in Mallorca; 80 ar Ph Rachel
Whiting/Pauline's apartment in Paris, designed by Marianne
Evennou www.marianne-evennou.com; 80 b Ph Mark Scott; 81 Ph
Benjamin Edwards/Katja Wöhr; 82 al Ph Benjamin Edwards/Katja
Wöhr; 82 bl Ph Benjamin Edwards/The home of conscious
entrepreneurs Gesine and Gerry Haag in Mallorca; 82 br Ph
Benjamin Edwards/Katja Wöhr; 83 Ph Benjamin Edwards/The home
of conscious entrepreneurs Gesine and Gerry Haag in Mallorca;
84–91 Ph Mark Scott; 92 al Ph Mark Scott; 92 bl Ph Lisa Cohen/
Anna McDougall's London home; 93 Ph Benjamin Edwards/The
Old Coastguard House – home of Martin and Jane Will; 94 Ph
Rachel Whiting/Niki Brantmark of My Scandinavian Home; 95 al
Ph Rachel Whiting/Karine Kong, founder and Creative Director of
online concept store Bodie and Fou, www.bodieandfou.com; 95 ar
Ph Benjamin Edwards/The home of conscious entrepreneurs Gesine
and Gerry Haag in Mallorca; 95 bl Ph Benjamin Edwards/The Old
Coastguard House – home of Martin and Jane Will; 95 br Ph Penny
Wincer and Gavin Kingcome; 96–103 Ph Benjamin Edwards/
Hannah Childs Interior Design, Old Lyme, CT; 104 al Ph Simon
Brown; 104 ar Ph Mark Scott; 104 b Ph Rachel Whiting/Jonathan
Lo; 105 Ph James Gardiner/Mark Hampshire and Keith Stephenson
of Mini Moderns; 106 al Ph Paul Massey/The home in Denmark of
Charlotte Lynggaard, designer of Ole Lynggaard; 106 bl Ph Mark
Scott; 106 br Ph Gavin Kingcome/William Yeoward; 107 Ph Gavin
Kingcome/William Yeoward; 108–113 Ph Mark Scott; 114 l Ph
Benjamin Edwards/The Ferryman's and The Saltbox are situated
on the Elmley Nature Reserve and available to rent

www.elmleynaturereserve.co.uk; **114 c** Ph Benjamin Edwards/The Old Coastguard House – home of Martin and Jane Will; **114 r** Ph Benjamin Edwards/The home of conscious entrepreneurs Gesine and Gerry Haag in Mallorca; **115 al** Ph Benjamin Edwards/The Old Coastguard House – home of Martin and Jane Will; **115 ar** Ph Benjamin Edwards/The Ferryman's and The Saltbox are situated on the Elmley Nature Reserve and available to rent www.elmleynaturereserve.co.uk; **115 b** Ph Catherine Gratwicke/Clapton Tram, the home of John Bassam in Hackney, available to hire via www.claptontram.com; **116 al** Ph Christopher Drake; **116 b** Ph Benjamin Edwards/The beach hideaway in Javea designed by Jessica Bataille www.jessicabataille.com; **117** Ph Benjamin Edwards/'Albany' in Port Isaac, designed by Nicola O'Mara and available to rent through www.uniquehomestays.com; **118–123** Ph Paul Massey/The Bartons' seaside home in West Sussex www.thedodo.co.uk; **124** Ph Simon Brown; **125 a** Ph Benjamin Edwards/The Shack is available as a shoot location www.lordshippark.com; **125 b** Ph James Gardiner/Jeska and Dean Hearne www.thefuturekept.com; **126 al** Ph Polly Wreford/The home of the Voors family in the Netherlands designed by Karin Draaijer; **126 ar** Ph James Gardiner/Rebecca Uth, creator of Ro; **126 b** Ph Christopher Drake; **127al** Ph Simon Brown; **127 ar** Ph Catherine Gratwicke/Caitlin and Samuel Dowe-Sandes of Popham Design; **127 bl** Ph Amy Neunsinger; **127 br** Ph Catherine Gratwicke/Caitlin and Samuel Dowe-Sandes of Popham Design; **128 a** Ph Jan Baldwin/owner of Westcott Design, Peter Westcott's cottage in Somerset; **128 b** Ph Rachel Whiting/Joy Cho – designer and blogger of Oh Joy!; **129 al** Ph Helen Cathcart/The home and studio of textile and product designer Donna Wilson in London; **129 ar** Ph Simon Brown; **129 bl** Ph Catherine Gratwicke/Caitlin and Samuel Dowe-Sandes of Popham Design; **129 br** Ph Polly Wreford/Siobhan McKeating's home in London; **130–131** Ph Jan Baldwin/The Normandy home of Fiona Atkins of Townhouse, Spitalfields; **132 l** Ph Debi Treloar/The home of Mark and Sally Bailey www.baileyshome.com; **132 c** Ph Polly Wreford/Foster House, the family home of Atalanta Bartlett and Dave Coote, available to hire through www.beachstudios.co.uk; **132 r** Ph James Fennell/Justin and Jenny Green, owners of Ballyvolane House; **133** Ph Debi Treloar/The home in Hampshire of Priscilla Carluccio; **134–141** Ph Debi Treloar/The home of Mark and Sally Bailey www.baileyshome.com; **142 a and b** Ph Debi Treloar/Okura; **143** Ph Benjamin Edwards/Archiects and homeowners Mette Fredskild and Masahiro Katsume; **144 a** Ph Debi Treloar/The home of Mark and Sally Bailey www.baileyshome.com; **144 bl** Ph Debi Treloar/Okura; **144 br** Ph Hans Blomquist; **145** Ph Debi Treloar/Okura; **146–151** Ph Mark Scott; **152** Ph Rachel Whiting/The home of interior journalist and blogger Jill Macnair in London; **153 a** Ph Mark Scott; **153 b** Ph Simon Brown; **154 al** Ph Polly Wreford/The home of the Voors family in the Netherlands designed by Karin Draaijer; **154 ar** Ph Gavin Kingcome; **154 bl** Ph Debi Treloar/Fog Linen Work; **154 br** Ph Simon Upton; **155 l** Ph Polly Wreford/Paul's

beach house in Sussex. Design www.davecootedesign.com; **155 r** Ph Benjamin Edwards/'Nautilus' is the home in Cornwall of James and Lisa Bligh www.uniquehomestays.com; **156–161** Ph James Gardiner; **162 a** Ph Catherine Gratwicke; **162 b** Ph Clare Winfield; **163** Ph Simon Brown; **163 inset** Ph Simon Brown; **164** Ph Simon Brown; **165 al** Ph Simon Brown; **165 bl** Ph Gavin Kingcome/William Yeoward; **165 r** Ph Gavin Kingcome; **166–171** Ph Mark Scott; **72 al** Ph Christopher Drake/Annie-Camille Kuentzmann-Levet's house in the Yvelines; **172 ar** Ph Keiko Oikawa and Amanda Darcy; **172 b** Ph Jan Baldwin/Fern Mallis' house in Southampton, Long Island; **173 al** Ph Emma Mitchell; **173 ar** Ph Paul Massey/The home in Denmark of Charlotte Lynggaard, designer of Ole Lynggaard; **173 b** Ph Christopher Drake/Florence and Pierre Pallardy, Domaine de la Baronnie, St Martin de Ré; **174 al** Ph Debbie Patterson; **174 ar** Ph Debbie Patterson; **174 b** Ph Christopher Drake/Annie-Camille Kuentzmann-Levet's house in the Yvelines; **175** Ph Jan Baldwin/The Normandy home of Fiona Atkins of Townhouse, Spitalfields; **176–183** Ph Earl Carter/Andrew Hoffman and Alex Bates' home on Fire Island; **184 a** Ph Eric Richards and Keith Scott Morton; **184 b** Ph Christopher Drake; **185 al** Ph Simon Brown; **85 ar** Ph Mark Scott; **185 bl** Ph Simon Brown; **185 br** Ph Simon Brown; **186** Ph Polly Wreford/The home of Mathilde Labrouche of Coté Pierre; **189** Ph Amy Neunsinger; **192** Ph Amy Neunsinger.

INDEX

Page numbers in *italics* refer
to illustrations

A
Allee, John 96
anemones 184, *185*
antiques *19*, 138, 158
aqua 90
aquamarine *41, 83, 92, 95*, 108, 128, *150*, 169, *169*
Arbuthnott, Nick and Vanessa 166–71
armchairs 84, 86, 146, *149*
  reupholstered *16, 19, 20, 42*
  slipcovers *43, 62, 99, 102*, 155, *156, 179, 183*
armoires 68, 69
Art Nouveau 25
Arts and Crafts 34, 137
Asian ikats 22
atmosphere, creating *127*
azure blue 158, *158, 166*, 169
azurite 142

B
Bailey, Mark and Sally 134–41
Baileys Home Store 134, 137–8
Bannon, Adrian *138*
Barton, Kate 118–23
Bataille, Jessica and Ivan 74–9
Bates, Alex and Andrew 176–83
bathrooms 46–9, 100, *100*, 121, *150*
  draped fabrics in 44, *45*
  flooring 128, *129*
  outdoor 120, *122*
  paint colours *125*
  tiles in 35, *48, 49*, 91, *91*
bathtubs *46*, 91, *91, 108, 111*, 120, *122*, 150
beach cabins 74–9
beach finds 74, *88*, 114, *114*
bed linen *23, 45*, 64, 65, *90, 111, 118, 120*, 121, 150
  quilts *16*, 25, *92, 94*, 100
bedrooms 92–5, 100, *100*, 108, 111, *111*, 121, *121*
  blue accents 90, *91, 92, 93, 95*
  decorative interest 44
  Delft tiles in 35
  guest bedrooms *45*, 120, *149*
  paint colours 125, *125*
  patterns in *64, 65, 92, 104, 120, 183*
beds *90, 94, 141*
  four-poster *16*, 108, *109, 118*
  vintage textiles 22
benches *33, 82, 99, 121, 137, 138*, 155, *172, 174*
biaude clothing *19, 20*
bleu de Fez 165
blinds/shades 22, 64, *92, 95*, 120
Blue Italian ware 165
books *26*, 31
bottles, glass *26*, 31, *41*, 65, 153
Boudin, Eugene 64

boutis 92
bowls *50, 52*, 56, *63, 77*
Breton inspirations 60–7
brickwork, exposed *41*, 43
bright blues *47, 68*
Bristol Blue glass 36
British Delftware 34

C
cabinets 69, *77*
  doors *49, 125*
  kitchen *31*, 90, 100, *152, 153*, 158, *158*
California ranch house 50–5
Cape Cod 90
Cape Floral Region 84–91
Caribbean blues *47, 62*
Carr, Maria 50–5
ceilings 124–7, 134, *150*
ceramics *77, 88*, 162–5
  blue-and-white *38, 41, 61, 63*, 64, *82*, 146, *149, 158*, 162–5
  Delft tiles 34–5, *48*, 153, *164, 171*
  Poole Pottery *41*, 43
cerulean blues 65
chairs 22, 69, 111, 155
  armchairs *16, 19, 20, 42*, 84, 86, 146, *149*
  bistro *52*, 100, *173*, 174
  covers *43, 60, 62, 99, 102*, 155, *156, 179, 183*
  folding *81, 88*
  outdoor *33, 82*
  seat pads *23, 92*, 155, *161, 174, 174*
chandeliers *52, 54*, 58, *59*, 111, 149
character, adding 68
check patterns *43*, 86, 90, *93, 104*, 152, *154*
chests of drawers *16, 20*, 68, 69
chevron patterns *104, 106*, 129
children's rooms 120
Childs, Hannah 96, 100
Chinese ceramics 162
chintz 22, *106*
coastal 26–33, 70–129
cobalt blue 53, 142, *149, 162*, 165
cobalt oxide 36
Coffey, Mike 176
Coffey houses 176–83
Cole & Son *127*
collections *41*, 43, *54*, 64, *77, 88*, 114–17
Colombo, Elena 26–33
colours, accent 53, 69, *90, 91, 92, 93, 95*, 158
concrete flooring 86, 88, 128, 153
cool blues 47
coral *31, 74, 117*
cork flooring 128
cottons 22, 25, *78, 106*, 140
country style *43*, 166–71
cupboards *54*, 68, *84, 88*
curtains 22, 25, *43, 52, 92*, 140

bedroom 64, *65*, 121
  kitchen *41*, 155, *158*
cushions/pillows 25, 64, *121, 138*, 146, *149*, 155, 156
  adding colour with *29, 78*, 90, 100, 158
  bedroom *16, 94*, 121
  outdoor *33*, 64, *81, 102, 176*
  vintage textiles 20, *20*, 22, *23, 53*
cutlery/flatware 82, *150*, 174

D
damasks 22, *106*
Danish summer cottage 156–61
Delft tiles 34–5, *48*, 153, *164, 171*
Delftware *169*
denim *16, 19, 20*, 144
dining rooms *41*, 43, *52, 74*, 88, *99*, 111, *121*, 152–5
displays 114–17
The Dodo 118–23
doors *54, 54, 62, 82, 83, 166, 173*
Dreamy Whites 54
dressers/hutches *41*, 69, 153, *164*
driftwood *31, 88*, 115
duck-egg blue 90, *129, 152*, 153
dyes 142–5

E F
East Sussex farmhouse 146–51
Ebner, Jennifer 96
enamelware 56–7, 88
fabrics *19, 43, 44, 45*, 92, *100*
  introducing colourful 155
  for outdoor spaces *81*, 82
  vintage 20, 22–5, *42*, 150
falu red 156, *156*
farmhouses 134–41, 146–51
Farrow & Ball *29, 149, 150*
feature lighting 58, *59*
Fetherstonhaugh, Sir Matthew *150*
Fez 165
filing chests *16, 20*
Fire Features *33*
Fire Island 176–83
fire pits *33*
fireplaces 34, 38, *53*, 60, 178
fisherman's cottage 74–9
flea markets 77
flooring 128–9
  concrete 128, 153
  laminate 50
  linoleum 49, 178, *181*
  natural floorboards 20, 100, *150*, 181
  painted *26*, 31, *65*, 120, *120, 121*, 128, *133*
  polished concrete *86*, 88
  tiled 49, *129*, 153
  vinyl 128, 153
flowers *50, 52*, 90, 155, *173, 174, 174*
  decorating with 184–5
  dried flowers *20*

floral motifs *43, 44, 45*, 104, *146*, 169
Fog Linen Work *138, 140, 141*
footstools 146, *149*
France: Breton inspirations 60–7
  textile design 22
  toiles de Jouy 25
French East India Company 22
French farmhouse style 50–5
furniture: garden 60, *62*, 81, *81, 82, 102, 172*, 174
  painted 68–9, 153
  see also chairs; tables, *etc*

G
garden retreats 172–5, 181
garlands *109, 113*
Gata de Gorgos 77
geometric patterns 25, 34, *64, 65, 79*, 92, 100, *104, 104*, 120, *121*, 129
Ghanaian textiles 137, *138, 141*
ginghams *43*, 152, 155
glassware 36–7, *41, 61, 63*, 64, 82, *115, 137, 158, 181*
  bottles *26*, 31, *41*, 65, 153
Great New England Hurricane (1938) *26*, 176
Greece 34, 62
Greenport house 26–33
grey blues 68, *152*
Grotto Bay beach house 108–13

H
hallways 96, *99, 127, 169*
height, room 125
hemp *16*, 115
historical influences 25
houseplants 184
hyacinth bulbs 184
hydrangeas *52, 173*, 184, *185*

I
ikat fabrics 22, 158, *161*
IKEA 158
India 144
indiennes 22, 25
indigo (colour) 19–20, *72*, 92, *102, 106*, 128, *133, 137, 138, 138, 140, 143*
indigo (dye) 9, 22, 142, 144, *145*
Indigofera tinctoria 142
Indonesian influences *111*
Industrial Revolution 34
Ione Valley ranch house 50–5
Islamic influences 34

J
Japan 144
  wabi-sabi 137
jasperware 165
Javea 75
Jorgensen, Else and Keld 156–61
Jouy-en-Josas 25

jugs/pitchers *41*, *45*, *50*, *54*, 56, 57, *146*, *169*
junk shops 28
jute sacking 137

K
Kabul *137*
kitchens 38, 152–5, *156*
    flooring 128, 153, *181*
    paint colours *31*, 125–6, 153
    small kitchens *77*, *84*
    tiles in 34, 35, *77*, 153, *154*, 158

L
laminate flooring 50, 128
lamps *31*, 58, 65, *77*, 158
lapis lazuli 142
lighting 58–9
    candelabras *88*
    chandeliers *52*, 54, 58, *59*, 111, 149
    feature lighting 58, *59*
    lamps *31*, 58, 65, *77*, 158
    natural 26, 64, 110, 125, 153, 156, *178*, *179*
    pendant lights 58, *59*
    spotlights 125
    task lighting 58
    vintage 58, *59*
linens 16, 22, 25, *25*, 78, 100, *100*, *133*, 140
linoleum flooring 49
Lithuanian linens 140
living rooms *29*, 35, 43, *43*, 53, 65, *79*, 100, 125, *161*, 169, *171*
London studio/showroom 16–21
Long Island homes 26–33, 96–103

M
Mallorcan designs *48*
mantelpieces 146, *149*, *179*
marble, blue-streaked 128
marine blues *31*, 47, 49
maritime influences 64, 67, 92, *114*, 116, *117*
Matisse blue 153, 178, *181*
medicine bottles *37*, 41
Mediterranean blues 47, 62
Mexican Talavera tiles 153
midnight blues 125, *125*
Mini Moderns *104*
Minton, Thomas 162, 165
mirrors 49, *52*, 115, 125, 149, *179*
Monet, Claude 64
Moore, Benjamin 100
Moroccan influences *48*, 153, 165
Morris, William 25, 137
mosaics 34, 91, *91*, 128
motifs 128
    Arts and Crafts 34
    Breton 60
    floral 43, 44, *45*, 104, *146*, 169
    nautical 92

N O
Nanking porcelain 162
napkins 36, *41*, *63*, 82, *99*, *149*, 150, 155
nature 25, *171*
nautical paraphernalia 92, 116, *117*
Normann Copenhagen 158
Oberkampf, Christophe-Philippe 25
Oi Soi Oi *161*
outdoor living 60, 61, 80–3, *156*

P
paint 29, 82, 125–6
panelled walls *31*, 48, 62, *62*, 111, 120
parasols 20, *138*
patterns 93, 104–7, 110, *164*, 169, *171*
    check 43, *86*, 90, *93*, 104, 152, *154*
    floral 43, 44, *45*, 104, *146*, 155, 169
    geometric 25, 34, 64, 65, *79*, 92, 100, 104, *104*, *120*, 121, 129
    gingham *43*, 152, 155
    stripes *45*, 46, *86*, 90, *93*, 100, *104*, *120*, 169
pebbles *31*, *88*, 114, *114*, *161*
Peru 9, 22
petrol blues 90
Picasso, Pablo 78
pigments 142–5
plants 50, *53*, *173*, 174, *174*, 184
plasterwork, scuffed 134
plates *41*, *63*, *77*
Pleasance, Lisette 146–51
Pole, Katharine 16–21
Poole Pottery *41*, 43
Popham Design *127*, *129*
porches *31*, *33*, *176*, *178*, 181, *183*
Portichol 74, *79*
Portmeirion *146*
pots, plant 184
powder blue 162
prairie living 50–5
proportion, room 125

Q R
quilts *16*, 19, 25, 92, *94*, 100
railway carriage/railroad car 118–23
ranch house 50–5
rattan *77*, *78*, 111, *176*
reclaimed materials 149–50
reclamation yards 120, *122*
recycled materials 22, 106
Renaissance artists 142
resin flooring 128
resist-dyeing techniques *137*
Romans 34, 144
room dividers 88
Ross-on-Wye farmhouse 134–41
rubber flooring 128
rugs *31*, 65, *77*, *88*, *91*, *99*, 100, *100*, 104, 106, 128, *133*, 158, *161*
Ruskin, John 137
rustic 130–85

S
Sabouret, Laurence and Yves 60–7
Sage Brick Co. 26, 28
St Malo 60–7
Saltaire, Fire Island 176–83
Sandy, Hurricane 181
Scandinavian style 47, 68, *156*
sea blues 65
sea glass 115
sea sponges 115
sea urchins *91*
seagrass carpets 121
seaweed 115
Sekine, Yumiko 140, *141*
Shaker style 68
Shaw, Mick 150
shells *31*, 64, 65, 114, *114*, 115, *118*
shelving *77*, *84*, *137*, 158
shingles *84*, 100, *102*, 181, *183*
shower curtains 44, *45*, *113*
shutters 54, *54*, 60, 74, 82, *83*, 95
Signac, Paul 64
silks 22
sky blues 68, 72, *86*, 121, *122*, 126, *154*, *171*
slate floor tiles 49
sofas 22, *53*, *138*
    covers *43*, 64, 65, *133*, *161*, *179*
    reupholstered in denim 16, *19*, 20
South African homes 84–91, 108–13
Spanish fisherman's cottage 74–9
splashbacks 48, *91*, 153
Spode, Josiah 165
staircases *19*, *99*, 100, 129, 168, *169*, *169*
starfish 109, 115
stools *53*, *77*, 78, 155, *172*
stripes 43, *45*, 46, *86*, 90, *93*, 100, 104, *120*, 169
studio/showrooms 16–21
Suffolk farmhouse 38–45
sunbeds 60, 62, 82, *172*

T
table runners 22, 36
tablecloths 23, *25*, 36, 38, *41*, *42*, *61*, *62*, 64, 82, 92, *99*, *149*, 150, 153, *174*, *174*
tables 38, 65, 68, 78, 88
    dining 150, 153
    farmhouse *31*, *52*, 54, 100
    outdoor 82, *83*, *172*, 174, *174*
tableware *41*, *43*, *77*, *164*
task lighting 58
teal blue 90, 121, *121*
terraces 60, *61*, 62, 64, *156*, *172*
terracotta tiles *77*, *77*, *79*
terrazzo tiles 128
textiles 23, 44, *45*, 78
    vintage 20, 22–5, *42*, 150
texture *77*, *100*, 111, *114*, *138*, 155
throws 22, *29*, *81*, *94*, 100, *141*, *183*
ticking 25, *43*, *53*, 104, *104*, *138*

tiles 49, *129*, 158, *158*, *161*
    Delft 34–5, *48*, 153, *164*, *171*
    handmade *48*, 128
    Mexican Talavera tiles 153
    Moroccan 153
    mosaic 34, 91, *91*, 128
    reclaimed tin 50, *53*
    terracotta *77*, *77*, *79*
    terrazzo 128
    vintage 128, *146*, *169*, *171*
Tisvildelej 156–61
toiles de Jouy 25
Tolix chairs 100
tongue-and-groove panelling 90, 111, 120
towels *46*, 60, *91*, *141*, 150, 155, *158*
transfer printing 34, 165
trompe l'oeil 127
Tuareg 20
turquoise *31*, *53*, *59*, 74, *75*, *77*, *79*, 82, *83*, 95, *127*, *154*, *174*

U V
ultramarine *48*, 142, 144
UNESCO World Heritage Sites 88
Uppark, West Sussex 150
utility/laundry rooms 149
vases 36, *37*, *164*, *174*, 184
Venetian traders 142
ventilation 88
views, framing 61, 64, 74
vintage 12–69
    enamelware 57
    fabrics 20, 21–5, *42*, 150
    lighting 58, *59*
    rugs 31
    tiles 128, *146*, *169*, *171*
    wallpaper *127*
vinyl flooring 128, 153

W Z
wabi-sabi 137, *141*, *143*
wallpaper 48, 64, 65, *104*, *127*, 149, 150
walls 124–7
    aged 134
    feature walls 125–6, 153
    panelled *31*, 48, 62, *62*, 111
    tongue-and-groove 90, 111, 120
    white 20
warm blues 47
Wedgwood *162*, 165
Wedgwood, Josiah 165
West Africa 144
white, shades of 110
Whitecross Farm 134–41
willow-pattern *41*, 149, *162*, *162*, *169*
window frames 49, *74*, *77*, 82, *83*, *122*, 149, 153, *166*, *173*
woad 142
wood-burning stoves *53*, *121*, *161*
woodwork, painting 49
Zen Buddhism *143*

ACKNOWLEDGMENTS

The author would like to thank all the owners who allowed us to photograph their beautiful houses, cottages and coastal retreats. Many of them generously provided information about the design and restoration work involved in creating the homes of their dreams, including insights into the history of the buildings and the inspirations behind their interior decoration and furnishings.

Heartfelt thanks are due to everyone at Ryland Peters & Small who was responsible for the editing and design of this book, in particular Sophie Devlin, Annabel Morgan and Megan Smith, and to Jess Walton for location research.